AGATHOS
THE ROCKY ISLAND

AND OTHER SUNDAY
STORIES AND PARABLES

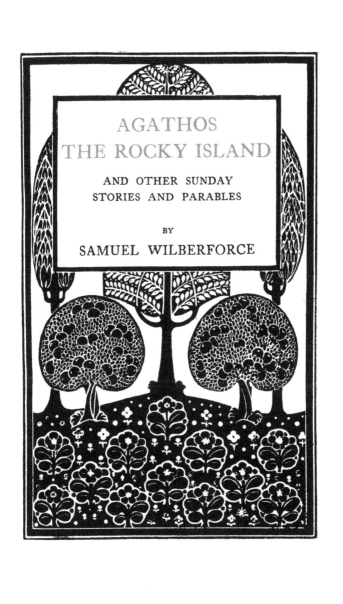

AGATHOS
THE ROCKY ISLAND

AND OTHER SUNDAY
STORIES AND PARABLES

BY

SAMUEL WILBERFORCE

"My speech shall distil as the dew, as the small rain upon the tender herb."—Deut. xxxii. 2.

"Even a child is known by his doings."—

Prov. xx. 11.

INTRODUCTORY NOTE TO
AGATHOS

THE author of these stories was the third son of the famous William Wilberforce. He was born in 1805; in 1830 he was made Rector of Brighstone in the Isle of Wight, from which he moved in 1840 to the rectory of Alverstoke. Five years later, he became Dean of Westminster; but within six months of his installation to the Deanery he was made Bishop of Oxford, and then, after nearly twenty-five years of strenuous and influential work, was translated to Winchester in 1869. He was killed by a fall from his horse in 1873.

These stories were written while the author was Rector of Brighstone, in 1839. On January 23 of that year he wrote to his brother, "I am just now very busy. I have engaged to write an introduction to, and revise, a set of sacramental prayers etc., which Burns is bringing out"—this was the admirable little volume called *Eucharistica*—"then I have my Oxford sermon to prepare, and divers other little things in hand." Of these "divers other little things" one was *Agathos, and other Sunday stories*, "which he mentions," his biographer tells us, "in his diary as finished on May 17, having been written in the first instance for his own children ; the apple tree in the garden, under which the most part of it was written, is still pointed out" (Ashwell *Life of Bp Wilberforce*, Vol. I. p. 140).

The little book had an immediate success. It ran through eight editions in three years. A twenty-third edition of it was published in 1861. This means that on an average at least one new edition was required every year till that date. It has been many times reprinted since, though the actual number of editions is difficult to ascertain. In whole or in part, it has been translated into French, German, Welsh, and Arabic,—perhaps into other languages also. The author had himself been brought up in one of the most pious of English households, and well knew how to meet the requirements of religious family life. Generations of English Christians have now learned to think with gratitude and affection of the book which taught them so much and in so pleasant a form in the days of their childhood.

In the present edition the short dialogues have been omitted which in some cases followed the narratives. It was thought that the meaning and application of the stories were sufficiently obvious without them, and that to some extent the dialogues detracted from the artistic effect of the book. In those cases where the story is based upon particular texts of Scripture, the reference has been prefixed in square brackets; where the reference is not in brackets, the author had himself prefixed it. An explanation of the Greek names has been added at the foot of the page. No other alteration, except occasionally in punctuation, has been made in this edition; even a few forms of words which appear to be incorrect, like *sunk* for *sank*, *laid* for *lain*, *Edonè* for *Hedonè*, have been left as the author wrote them.

A. J. MASON.

PEMBROKE COLLEGE,
  CAMBRIDGE.
 25 *February*, 1908.

CAMBRIDGE UNIVERSITY PRESS
Cambridge, New York, Melbourne, Madrid, Cape Town,
Singapore, São Paulo, Delhi, Mexico City

Cambridge University Press
The Edinburgh Building, Cambridge CB2 8RU, UK

Published in the United States of America by Cambridge University Press, New York

www.cambridge.org
Information on this title: www.cambridge.org/9781107671690

First published 1908
First paperback edition 2013

A catalogue record for this publication is available from the British Library

ISBN 978-1-107-67169-0 Paperback

CONTENTS

PREFACE

THE following allegories and stories have been actually related by the Author to his children on successive Sunday evenings. He began the practice with the earnest desire of combining some sort of occupation suitable to the Lord's-day with something which might amuse his little ones. Few parents can, he thinks, have failed to feel the want which he would here hope in some measure to supply.

On the one hand, if the conversations and employments of Sunday are not early marked as different from those of other days, how is it possible that our children can grow up with a deeply-rooted reverence for its holiness? On the other hand, if the day is one which they remember only for its dulness, how can children grow up in the love of this blessed season? "Everlasting droopings[1]" their young hearts least of all will "bear." And if on other days they are used to amusing employments, if they love (and all children should be made to love them) the times of relaxation in which they

[1] Herbert's "Country Parson," cxxvii.

see their parents as friends, and in some sort companions, what else can happen, if on this day all amusement be banished, and all interest removed, but that they will grow insensibly to feel the Lord's-day a weariness? But if the week-day's tale is changed for the Sunday story; if the child is really interested in it, he learns, even unawares, to separate in his own mind the first day of the week from its common days; and that by a pleasurable separation.

Such has been, to a remarkable degree, the effect of the first telling of these stories in the Author's family; and such he cannot help hoping may be more widely their effect when they are given to the public. The questions at the close of each[1] are designed as tracks, not as grooves, and they may easily be multiplied or reduced in number, according to the judgment of the parent, or the age and intelligence of the child. Some of them are the very answers he received from his children.

One word more should be said about the plan of these narratives. The Author's greatest care has been, while interweaving in them as much instruction as he could about the Holy Scriptures, its allegories, and some of its most striking narratives, to keep as far as possible

[1] They are omitted in this edition.

from all lowering down of holy things, or making the mysteries of the faith common and cheap to childish imaginations. Against this most dangerous evil, which appears to him to infest and poison many of the current religious books for children, he begs here most earnestly to protest, as against that which is laying unawares the foundation of untold evils, in accustoming the mind to look curiously, and with levity, on things which man must never approach but with humiliation and adoration. "Put off thy shoes from off thy feet; for the place whereon thou standest is holy ground." This should be from the first the temper carefully wrought into our children's minds, if we would have them approach God with acceptance.

To teach them to think boldly of mysteries, in the vain hope of explaining to their childish minds what in the fulness of their highest understanding they can never truly comprehend, may make them shrewd and forward questioners, but cannot make them meek and teachable disciples.

It only remains further to say, for what age these stories are intended. The Author's children reach from five to nine years old, and are of ordinary powers of comprehension. Of these, the eldest has been fully interested by the simplest

3   I—2

narratives, and the youngest has understood
the most difficult. All the applications of the
allegorical tales they of course will not understand at first; but in the Author's judgment, this
is the very excellence of allegorical instruction.
The minds of children may be fatally dwarfed
by never having presented to them anything but
that which they can understand without effort;
whilst it is exceedingly difficult to devise anything which shall at the same time attract their
attention and stretch their faculties. It is exactly
this want which allegory supplies: the story
catches the attention of the youngest; glimpses
of the under-meaning continually flash into their
minds, and whilst it is difficult to say exactly
how much they have fully understood, it is clear
that it has been enough to give them interest,
and arouse their faculties.

May God hereby bless some of the tender
lambs of His fold.

ADVERTISEMENT

TO THE SECOND EDITION

THE rapid sale of a numerous edition of this little work not only proves the existence of the want which it is intended to supply, but is also a gratifying mark of the kindness with which the attempt has been received.

On one point the Author has been requested to say a single word in explanation of his plan. Some of the stories are gathered from Holy Scripture, and yet do not adhere in every particular to the letter of the Bible narrative: and he has been requested to explain the principle of such variations. They consist, then, he would say, in every case, of the mere marking out of lines which the general sketch of Scripture appeared to him to contain :—the filling up for his young readers of the picture, which is set before them there in outline merely. Thus, for instance, in the ninth story, David is represented as slaying the lion and the bear in a time of snow, though this is not mentioned in the passage which records the fact. But in another chapter we find the slaying of a lion especially recorded

5

ADVERTISEMENT

with the addition that it was "in the time of snow" :—2 Sam. xxiii. 20; and this seeming to point out the season of the year at which such beasts were wont to leave their more retired haunts, it is introduced to perfect the picture which the brief narrative of Scripture sketches only in outline.

No further liberty has been taken with the letter of God's word; and this does not, the Author trusts, exceed the just and necessary limits of exposition.

SUNDAY STORIES

I

AGATHOS, OR, THE WHOLE ARMOUR OF GOD

[Ephesians vi 11—17]

THERE was once a brave king whose country
was visited by a very fierce and deadly dragon.
The king chose out therefore some of his best
soldiers, and sent them into that part of the land
where this dragon was doing so much mischief.
Before they went, he said to them—"You all
know that I have fought with this dragon, and
conquered and smote him, though he put forth
all his rage and power against me. All my
faithful followers must tread in my footsteps;
they must overcome as I overcame, and then
they shall sit upon the steps of my throne.
Therefore I send you out to fight with this
monster, and my strength shall go forth with
you in the battle. Be therefore upon your guard.

If you remember my words, and call upon my name in the time of danger; and above all, if you take and use boldly all the armour I have provided for you; then the dragon can never hurt you. But if he finds you unprepared—if he comes upon you without your armour, then he will certainly set upon you and slay you."

The soldiers promised to be upon their guard, and set off in high spirits into the land where the evil beast lay. When first they came there, they kept their guard very diligently, and always wore their armour. They never all slept at once; but some always watched whilst the others rested. It was a fine sight to see these brave men in their shining armour, marching up and down the land, and all the people safe and happy because the king's army was keeping guard. It was a fine sight to see them early in the morning, when some one or two had long been watching whilst the others slept, and they were now about to change turns; it was a fine sight to see how the brave men would wake up refreshed by sleep, and put on carefully their armour, and try their swords to see that they were keen and sharp; and then kneel down and pray, and call upon the name of their prince, and then go out to keep their guard against the evil dragon.

This was a noble sight to see, but, alas, it

did not last: all the time they watched, they never saw the dragon. All went on quietly round them. The farmers ploughed their lands, and the reapers were soon about to reap in the harvest; there were marriages, and feasts, and pleasures, and business; and the soldiers began to think that perhaps after all it was but an empty tale that had been spoken of the dragon, and to forget their master's word about watching and standing fast. The weather, too, grew very hot and sultry, and their arms seemed heavier than they had ever done before. "What," said one, "can be the use of always wearing this heavy lumbering helmet? The sun heats it till it scorches me up; and no one ever sees this terrible dragon. I shall leave my helmet in the tent; it will be time enough to run and fetch it when I see the dragon coming." So said another of his breastplate; and another found his shield so troublesome and cumbrous, that he laid it up in the tent; and the ground had grown so hot and sandy that they found their brazen sandals tire and burn their feet, so they cast them too away, and sauntered about, some here and some there; to this feast, and to that wedding; some without this part of their armour, and some without that, until you could scarcely have known them, unless you looked very close

9

to find the king's mark, to be the soldiers of the king, who had looked so bright and terrible, when their prince sent them out with their armour and his warnings into the far battle-field.

One indeed there was of the troop, who would not give in to their ways; Agathos[1] was his name, and sorely was he grieved by the sight of careless comrades. Often and often did he remind them of their prince's caution, and tell them that the enemy was surely near, although as yet they saw him not; that their prince could not be mistaken, for that he himself had fought with the dragon, and knew how terrible he was. The rest also laughed and jeered at the brave man, and called him coward, and many other hard names, because he would not do as they did. But he meekly put up with it all; and neither their hard words, nor the hot sun by day, making him often faint, nor the weary sands over which he had to march, nor the cold wet dews of the night, could make Agathos lay aside the armour which his prince had bid him wear; or to take off the brazen sandals from his swollen feet, or cease watching carefully all the night through.

All this went on for some time longer, and the hard words of the idle soldiers grew harder and harder as they became more and more sure

[1] " Agathos" is the Greek for " good."

that they should never see their enemy. But just when they thought themselves most safe the danger was at hand. For now there were fearful sights to be seen, if one could have been by to witness them. One of the soldiers was coming home about this time from a great feast, at which he had been. There had been mirth, and merriment, and songs, and dances, and the soldier had taken off his armour; and now he was walking lightly home to his tent, through the pleasant summer evening air. He was thinking of the merry party which had just broken up, and what a happy life he was leading, and pitying Agathos, whose fears and scruples kept him always pacing about the tent in his heavy armour. But just as these thoughts passed through his mind, he heard a strange rustling noise in a wood upon his right hand; and in an instant, as quick as lightning, the dreadful form of the fierce dragon stood before him. His knees knocked together as he felt at his side for the keen sword his prince had given him: but it was not there. The dragon was making at him, and in his terror he called upon his king, but something seemed to tell him it was too late now; that he would not bear the burden of his armour, and therefore that there was no one to help him—and he turned to fly, but the place

seemed all beset with piercing darts which the
dragon had cast upon the ground; and he had
thrown away the king's sandals of brass; so his
feet failed him and he fell upon the ground, and
the evil beast devoured him.   So it was with one
and another, and their companions missed them;
and at first they wondered why they came not
home; then they looked sad and grave for a
while, when they spoke of them, but soon they
feasted, and ate, and drank just as merrily, and
forgot their armour and their prince's word, and
knew not that danger was at hand.

But the dragon, who had gained courage by
all these victories over the soldiers of the prince
whom he feared, now thought he might attack
the camp itself, and slay all his enemies at once.

Long time he lay hid in the wood bordering
on the camp: for he saw Agathos walking up
and down, and keeping guard as he had done
always, and he saw his biting sword hanging
at his side, and his huge shield with a bright
red cross upon it hung over his shoulder, and
he remembered his battle with the prince, and
he feared.

But when the next noon-day was come, and
Agathos, who had watched long, had gone into
his tent and laid down to get a little needful
sleep, whilst his companions were all around the

tent, then the dragon thought that his time was
come, and with a mighty yell he rushed forth
from the cover of the wood, and fell, tooth and
nail, upon the soldiers, tearing some with his
cruel claws, fixing his iron teeth in others, and
stinging many to death with his poisonous tail.
Then was there a great cry all through the camp
for the forgotten armour; and one seized a sword
and made against the dragon for a moment,
but because he had no helmet, whilst he was
aiming a blow, the dragon darted his claws
upon his head, and he fell down slain ; and by
this time another had rushed up with a helmet
buckled on, and a sword in his hand, and he
fought longer, and gave the dragon a wound,
whereupon he cast forth his burning sting, which
reached all around to his loins, and as there was
no armour girded on them, he, too, fell down
and died.   Then started up another, and he
seemed wellnigh armed, but in his hurry he
could not wait to seek for the shield which
he had thrown carelessly aside; and so when
he joined in battle with the dragon, and smote
at him with his good sword, and had wounded
him somewhat, and the dragon could not seize
upon his helmeted head, or sting his well greaved
loins; suddenly he saw the evil one cast fiery
darts out of his wicked talons, and these his

sword could not stop, and he had no shield on which to catch them, and so they lighted upon him and pierced through his armour, and he fell down slain; and the next was overcome, because in the hot fight, when his shield was knocked aside for a moment, his breast was without its breastplate, and so he was wounded to the death; and another fell through the broken darts with which the ground was strewn, because he had come forth from his tent without his sandals; and now the dragon was triumphing in the greatness of his strength, and thinking soon to swallow up the prince's army.

But the noise had woke Agathos from a sweet holy dream, which had been cheering his sleep. He thought he saw his prince standing near him just as he had been when he fought himself with the dragon; blood dropped from his hands and his feet, but the dragon was trodden under them; and he thought his master looked upon him with his own look of strength and kindness, and said, "Good and faithful servant," "thou shalt go upon the lion and the adder, the young lion and the dragon shalt thou tread under thy feet; and fear not, for I am with thee." Even with these words sounding in his ears he was roused by the cry of his companions, and the fierce voice of the dragon. Then, as he had always expected his attack, Agathos was not startled or hurried; but, springing from the ground, he girded his bright sword upon his thigh; and his breastplate, and his greaves, and his sandals were all bound upon him in their places, for even in sleep he would not cast them off; and he fitted his helmet on his head, and drew his arm through the handle of his shield; and then he knelt down upon the ground, and called upon the Lord, and thought upon his prince, and rushed out into the battle. When the enemy saw him coming, he left trampling on the slain and moved on to meet him. Then was there a dreadful battle between that good soldier of his Lord and the fierce enemy. More than once was Agathos beaten on his knees, and could but just keep up the good shield of faith against the storm of blows and showers of fiery darts which the evil one poured forth; yet even as he touched the ground it seemed as if new strength came into him, and he lifted up the feeble knees, and smote with a mightier strength against the accursed destroyer. The battle still was raging when the sun went down: and the good soldier was wellnigh sinking, when he gathered all his might into one strong blow, and calling out aloud upon the name of his prince, he smote the dragon so fiercely that he

15

uttered a piercing cry and fled quite away, and
left him to himself. Then was Agathos right
glad, and he kneeled down and prayed, and gave
thanks; and over the battle-field he could see
the form of his master coming to him amongst
the dews of the evening; and he heard his voice,
and he saw his countenance, and his happy
dream was more than true, and he dwelled for
ever in the presence of his prince.

II

THE RAVENS IN THE FAMINE

[1 Kings xvii 1—6]

THE spring-time was come, and the birds had all built their nests, and sat upon their smooth round eggs till they had hatched them; and now they were busy flying here and there, and running along the ground, some picking up seeds, and some catching flies, and some seizing every worm which put his head above the damp ground; and all carrying them off as fast as possible to feed their young ones, as they were taught to do by the instinct which God Almighty had given them. It was a busy, happy scene. Cheerful too it was to the ear as well as to the eye; for sometimes they stopped from their labour to sing a song of praise to the good God who has made this happy world.

Amongst these birds there were two great black ones called ravens. These flew to a town a long way off, and there they lighted by a great shop, where a man was busy selling bread and meat to the people who came to buy. The man

threw them each a lump of bread and piece of
meat for the sport of the people round: and
the birds took them in their strong beaks, and
flew straight away with them—and the people
clapped their hands and shouted. But they were
all surprised when just at night the same birds
came again to the same place, and seemed to
ask for more, and then flew away with what
was given them, just as they had done in the
morning. The next day they came again as
soon as the shop was open, and when they had
got what they wanted, away they flew with it,
and were seen no more till night, and then again
they only stayed till some bread and meat was
given them ; and then nobody saw more of
them. Many persons tried to watch them ; they
must have, it was thought, some great nest near,
and they took all this with them to feed their
nestlings.

But perhaps these people were quite wrong ;
for God, who has taught birds in general to feed
their young ones, has before now taught them
a different lesson. So it was at that time of
which we read in the Bible, when he taught
ravens to feed one of the Prophets. If any one
could have flown with them and seen all their
doings, it would have been a strange sight.
How they got the meat we do not know; but

we know that any one who could have flown
with them would have seen that as soon as they
got it they flew straight away with it to another
country. Then they passed over a land where
everything was dry and burnt up for want of
rain. It had not rained for a whole year, and
all the brooks were dry. The little streams which
had leapt from stone to stone were drunk in by
the thirsty ground, and their murmuring voice
was no more heard; the corn was parched up
and would not grow; the grass was dried and
withered; the cattle had eaten it quite close
down to the dusty earth, and then had grown
thinner and thinner till they had died. Men's
faces had grown thin and sharp, and their eyes
looked hungrily out of their sunk cheeks; and
their tongues were dry, and swelled with thirst;
and they walked about, here and there, looking
for food and for water, and they could not
find any.

"There was a great famine in that land."

Yes, there was a great famine. The people
of the land had sinned against God, and he had
bid "the clouds that they should rain no rain
upon it." And if you could have flown with
those ravens, you would have heard a great
voice of sadness, and sighing, and sorrow, rising
from all that land as they flew over it.

THE RAVENS IN THE FAMINE

But where do you think the ravens were flying to? They flew over all that land till they came to a cave in the side of a high sandy hill; and if you could have looked into that cave you would have seen, not a nest of young ravens, but one man sitting, or standing, or kneeling by the side of a little brook that rose high up in the cave, and sunk just below in the thirsty land, so that no one else knew of it.

Perhaps you might have seen this good man kneeling down and lifting up his hands towards the sky, and saying, " O Lord God, who hast kept me hitherto, and ordered the wild ravens to feed me, take Thou care of me this day, for Thou art my God, and I am Thy servant."

And then the mouth of the cave was darkened for a moment; it was by the wings of the great ravens, as they flew in and laid down the meat and the bread before the good man's feet; and he would rise and gather a few dry sticks to dress the meat at the cave's mouth, and drink some of the clear spring water, and then kneel down again to thank his God who had taught the ravens to fly all over the starving country to bring it to him in this lonely cave.

III

THE MAN IN THE DUNGEON

[Acts xii 1—17]

THERE was a deep dungeon—its walls were all green and stained with the damp which had long hung on them; its floor was made of cold rough stones. It had one small window, across which were thick iron bars, and it was so narrow and so high up, that hardly any light came from it to the floor. It was night, and all was quite still and silent there: even in the day, no cheerful sound came into that sad place; not even a bird's song was ever heard there; scarcely even a fly could ever be seen in it: but now it was night, and dark, and silent, except when now and then the moving of chains was heard on that dungeon's floor. For a man was lying there chained, by chains which went round his wrists. But his chains made no noise now, for he was lying still: he was asleep; sleeping as quietly, and breathing as gently, as if he were a child. How could he be sleeping so gently? Did he know where he was? Yes, he well knew: and he knew too, that when the sun rose the next morning, and woke so many persons all around him to their daily work, or to their daily pleasures, that it would see him led out of that prison to be put to a cruel death; for that the very next morning he was to be killed. Then surely he must have been some very wicked man; for why else should he be in that dungeon, and why else should he be about to be killed? You would the more have thought so if you could have seen all; for you would have seen that he was chained to two soldiers, who lay on each side of him, with their weapons ready to slay him if he were to move. Fierce, evil-looking men they were, of dark and savage faces; they were asleep, but even in their sleep they looked angry and cruel. The gate of the dungeon too was barred and locked, and there were four other soldiers asleep outside it; and beyond them again was a great iron gate fast closed, so that surely he must be a very wicked and desperate man whom they are guarding with this strength and care. And yet, if you could look into his face, you would see him sleeping quietly and calmly. A little child upon the knees of his mother could hardly sleep more gently. And could he sleep so if he were indeed a wicked man? Could his conscience be asleep when he was thus deep in the dungeon, and death coming so near to him? No doubt he could not: no doubt that his sleep could not have been what it was, unless God had been with him there: for he was a holy man, one who did indeed love God, one who had followed Jesus Christ when He lived upon this earth, and whom with eleven others Jesus Christ had trusted to govern His church, now that He had ascended into heaven. He had been thrown into that dungeon because he loved Jesus Christ, and believed in Him, and would speak about Him among people who hated Him; and so their wicked king had laid hold on him, and cast him into this dungeon, and was about to put him to death the very next day. He seemed now given over, for no one else was to be seen in that dungeon but the poor man in chains, and the fierce soldiers to whom he was bound. But there was another there; there was one who watched over him; who kept him from all harm; who gave him that sweet sleep; who heard when he prayed, and was ever ready to help him—Jesus Christ was there.

There was in that town another room, not a very large one, and yet there were many persons in it. It was now late at night, but still they stayed there. There were some men and some women—what are they doing? They are praying to God, calling on the name of Jesus Christ, begging Him to save His servant Peter, and not to let him, like St James, be put to death by Herod. They prayed very earnestly, and no doubt their prayers were heard. Perhaps it is as an answer to their prayers, that the chained prisoner sleeps so peacefully; for he looks as if some happy vision or dream came to him as he slept. Perhaps he is dreaming of the time when he was a boy, and went with his father upon the lake of Gennesaret as a fisherman.

Perhaps he dreams of the first time he went; how pleased he was to go; how the bright moon shone, and the little waves rippled round the boat, as it shot with its dark shadow through the moonlight, and left a troubled path on the waters where it had passed. Is that his father's voice calling him? Is that the moonlight round him? See, he starts in his sleep and opens his eyes; he looks like a man who hardly knows whether he is well awake, or still in a dream. What is the light around him? there was never moonlight in the dungeon, and he is there, and not by the sea of Galilee. And what is this light, brighter, and yet softer far than any moonlight? It is so clear that he can see every corner of the dungeon, and yet so mild that it does not dazzle his eyes, which had been so long in the darkness. And what is that voice which says to him, "Arise up, quickly," as kind as his father's in his dream, and yet a real sounding voice? The soldiers too beside him, why do they sleep on? He looks up, and he sees a form he knows not. Is it one of God's angels? the light seems to beam from him: either he must be a holy angel, or all this is a beautiful dream. But he does as the voice bids him; he rises up, and the chains fall off from his hands; they clanked and rung as they fell upon the ground, but the soldiers did not stir: the hand of one of them was upon the hilt of his sword; in a moment surely it would be drawn, and Peter slain: but no, the fierce man slept on, and Peter bound on his sandals, and followed the angel. He passed the first gate, for it opened for them; the keepers lay around it, but no man stirred, and it shut again behind them. They came to the second; it too is left behind. Surely it must be a dream. But now they stand before the iron gate; its heavy weight hangs always stiffly on its rusty hinges, and many men can only just slowly and scarcely force it open with a great creaking and noise. It too opens of its own accord, and they pass through it into the open air. It was a very pleasant feeling; that first breath of the open summer night breeze upon Peter's forehead, which had grown damp and cold in the dark wet dungeon. Surely it must be more than a dream. He looked round for the angel who brought him forth, but he was gone—gone as he came, unseen and unknown by man, save when God would have him seen. Perhaps he stood near him still, though he could be seen no longer. Peter stands doubtful for a moment. Then all the truth comes surely on his mind, and he knew that "the Lord had sent His angel, and delivered him out of the hands of Herod, and from all the expectation of the people of the Jews." And he went to that room where the servants of the Lord were together praying, and they would scarcely believe when they heard that Peter was there. But he went in and told them what great things the Lord had done for him; and he and they feared the Lord together, and trusted in Him more and more.

IV

THE CHILDREN AND THE LION

[1 Peter v 8]

THERE was once a Father who had two
children whom he loved exceedingly. They were
a little girl and boy, and they were good and
obedient children. For many years, ever since
they were born, they had lived in the middle
of a great town, and had never seen the open
fields and the beautiful flowers, and birds, and
woods, except sometimes when their father took
them out in a carriage with him for an hour or
two; and those were happy times. One day,
when the little girl was seven, and the boy nine
years old, their father called them to him, and
said to them, "My dear children, I am going to
take you away from this house in which you have
been used to live, and to take you into another
house where you will have a beautiful garden, in
which you can play about amongst the flowers,
and hear the birds sing all day long, and see
the bright butterflies which you have seen when
I have taken you out in the carriage."

How pleased the little boy and girl must
have been to go to such a beautiful house, from
the midst of the dark town where they had lived
before.

THE CHILDREN AND THE LION

Yes, they were greatly pleased; and when
the next day they came to this new house, and
looked out of its windows, and saw the green
grass looking fresh and bright, and gay butterflies
flying over it up and down, and the painted
feathers of all sorts of birds which flew in and
out of the bushes, or stayed to warble in the
thickets, they longed to run straight out of doors
and sing too, they were so happy, and thought
that they should never tire of gathering the
flowers, and playing with the bright yellow
gourds which they could see growing here and
there in the beds, and watching the birds and
butterflies. But just as they were running out,
their father called them to him with a very grave
face, so grave as to be almost sad, and said to
them, "My dearest children, before you go into
that beautiful garden, listen well to what I am
going to tell you. In that garden there is a fierce
and hungry lion, who is always walking up and
down it, to find some one to devour. There
are reasons, which you cannot understand, why
I cannot turn this lion out; and why, much as
I love you, I have yet brought you to live in this
garden, near such a savage beast; but if you
will remember my words, he can never hurt you.
What you must do is this: keep in mind that
he is ever near you, that he is waiting to spring

28

on you; and when the sun is the brightest, and
the birds the gayest, and all is most beautiful
around you, and you are the happiest yourselves,
then think that he is near you, and watch
carefully lest he should spring on you unseen;
for if, when you see him, you call on me to help
you, you will find me always near you, and he
will fly away from you. Do not stay to think
how I can hear you when you do not see me,
but call at once on me, and I shall be always
by your side, and you will be safe. But if in
your play you cease to watch for the lion, and
so are not ready to call on me, he will creep
close to you when you least expect it, and spring
on you and devour you."

The children looked very grave and thoughtful; each took the other's hand, and they walked
quite sadly down into the garden, trembling and
afraid, as though thinking that at every turn the
great lion would spring out upon them. But they
saw nothing of him; and as the birds hopped
round them, and the gay butterflies floated up
and down in the air, and the sun sparkled in
the stream that ran amongst the flowers, they
began to forget that there was such a thing as
a lion in the world; and soon they were playing
and laughing as merrily and loud as if they
had never heard that he was near them. But

just when they were the gayest, they heard their father's voice, saying, sadly and seriously, "*Remember!*" They started and looked round, but they could not see him: the voice seemed to come from the air; but the little girl thought directly of the lion; and as she looked into the bushes, which were quite white with their bright blossoms, she saw something creeping softly towards her, and in a moment her eyes were fixed on the fierce fiery eyes of the savage lion. She had hardly breath left to call upon her father, but at the first call he stood by her side; and she could see the lion turn from her, and spring away and hide himself in the thicket. Her father took her in his arms, and told her not to fear, for that she was quite safe in his keeping; and he bid her remember, that if she had not watched, and seen the lion, and called on HIS name, the evil beast would have sprung upon her, and she would have been his prey.

Day after day passed away, and the children became more and more watchful, and even in their sport and play they were sober and mindful of the lion; and when he was stealing near to them, they called always on their father, and he ever stood beside them, and saved them from his fangs.

V

THE STORM AT SEA

[Jonah i, ii]

A LARGE ship lay near the shore; she was
waiting for the wind; for all her cargo was on
board. The sea, which had been long as calm
as a great looking-glass, began to be ruffled
over here and there as the flaws of wind fell
upon it, and the little waves began to rise upon
it, looking very bright where the sun fell upon
their sparkling tops, and quite black and dark
where they curled away from his shining; and
as they followed one another on to the pier, they
broke against and ran up it, throwing up a little
salt spray, through which the sun shone in many
colours like a rainbow.

When the wind began to rise, every one was
busy on board the ship. The sailors were running
about, pulling the ropes, and shaking out the sails,
and drawing up the anchor; and the captain was
walking here and there, and seeming to think
that they could never work hard enough, or get
the ship quick enough ready to sail out to sea
whilst the pleasant breeze lasted. However, the
sailors laboured, and all was just ready, when
a man came down to the sea-shore and jumped

into a boat which lay there, and called to the
sailors near to row him out to the ship, before
she should sail away. He had but just time to
reach her: he got alongside just as she began
to cut the water with her keel, and he begged
the captain to take him on board, and he would
pay for his passage. After a few words it was
settled between them; the boat pulled back to
the shore, and the stranger was standing on the
deck of the vessel, watching the windows and
the people and the houses, as they grew less
and less every moment, until they could scarcely
be seen the one from the other.

There were many things to do as the ship
sailed on, and the captain and the sailors had
not much time to look about them, or they would
have wondered whom they had got on board.
He was dressed in rough hairy clothes, and did
not look like a merchant, or a sailor, or a soldier.
He did not seem a rich or great man; and
yet if you looked near into his face, there was
something in it which made you look again and
again. He seemed very full of thoughts; and
these many thoughts had made many deep
furrows in his face, and when he was pleased,
as he was when he found that he had caught
the ship, his face was lighted up with a very
great joyfulness. But altogether he seemed very

sad now. He hardly spoke to any one, and he looked often out into the air and the sky, as if he saw strange things there, which were seen by no one beside. When any one spoke suddenly near him, he gave a great start, and seemed half ready to answer, as if he were expecting some one to call him. However, he was not much noticed, for every one was busy except himself, and had little time for looking at him. The sailors indeed would shrug their shoulders sometimes, and whisper to one another when he was amongst them; but for the most part he went on his way and they on theirs, and they said little to each other.

For the first day the breeze favoured them, and they were getting well on with their voyage. The sun rose clear the next day, and the pleasant breeze held up. The anxious face of the captain grew smoother, and he had a friendly word for the sailors when they came near him. Every one was busy in their work. You might see him walking, as sailors do, up and down the deck, talking to the chief of his crew under him. Perhaps they were talking about the cargo he had got on board, and what would be the state of the market at Tarshish, and how much he should make by the wheat and the fine cloth he had got on board; and whether he should

M. 33 3

find plenty of "gold and silver, and ivory and apes" at Tarshish, which he could bring back again in his ship to Joppa. Perhaps they talked about the strange man who had come on board, and what could be his business. "He paid his fare, but he does not seem like a merchant; and he eats little and speaks to no one; and all last night the sailors say he never slept, but seemed like a man in whom some spirit dwelt." So perhaps they talked, as the ship cut gaily through the waters, bounding like a spirited horse over the tossing waves.

But when the sun was past the middle of the sky, and he began to sink towards the sea, a belt of thick clouds might be seen stretching along to the eastward. If a man watched them closely, he might see that they were creeping up the sky. You might see that they would soon be up with you,—those sky-travellers. And so they were; another hour spread them all over the heaven, and now the sun was getting near the sea; and the light was growing dim and grey.

"We shall have but an ugly night of it, from the look of the sea and sky," was the captain's judgment, and nobody thought him wrong. Already the wind was sighing over the sea, and whistling among the cords: and hark! what crack of the sail was that? "We shall not long

34

be able to carry any sail at all." They were right; the wind grew into a storm, the storm grew into a hurricane: it was a fearful night; black and rough and roaring was the sea, and the poor ship strained and tossed as she drove along before the wind, like a bubble on the wave-top. At last the grey light of the morning began to give a leaden colour to the sky and the waves, but no help came with it. The wind only got higher and higher, and the waves tossed more and more fearfully, till they thought the ship would be broken by their force.

Then the captain bid the sailors bring up the costly merchandise of which he had hoped to make so good a sale, and throw it into the sea to lighten the ship, for "we had better lose it," he said, "than be all sunk together." So they brought it up, beautiful ears of wheat from Judæa, and bales of fine cloth of blue from Tyre, and they threw them into the sea, and the wild waves tossed them up as if they were playing with them, and then yawned, opened, and sucked them in, and they saw them no more. But still the storm did not abate, and they thought that soon the ship must go to pieces.

Now the captain and his men were heathen people, and did not know the true God; so they said in their heathen way, that they wondered

35   3—2

which of the gods had sent this storm: for they thought that there were many gods; and they began to pray every man to the god whom they most fancied. Then said one of the sailors, " Where is the strange passenger in the rough garments, and why is not he praying with us?" So they sought for him, and they found him down below fast asleep; so worn out by watching, that he had fallen asleep at last, and slept all through that fierce night-storm which had kept all the rest so busy and so full of fear.

It was a strange sight to see how the man awoke: how he started and looked around him, and seemed more moved than any, as soon as he was woke from that sound sleep. Then they all prayed unto their gods, and the stranger prayed by himself. No one heard his prayers, but it seemed that he was very earnest. Yet still the storm ceased not, but it tossed and roared worse and worse.

The captain's voice was then heard, and he said, " We must cast lots and see for whose sake this dreadful storm has come upon us." So they made lots, and began to cast them as best they could, in such a troubled state. And now all men marked the stranger, for his knees smote together, and his face was pale, and his eyes were fixed in the air, as if there sat always

before them some terrible thing which no one
else beheld. Soon the lots were given out, and
the strange man was taken. Then said the
captain to him, "Tell us who thou art, from what
country, and of what business, and what doing of
thine has brought this trouble upon us?"

Then was it wonderful to look upon that man,
for he who had been so terrified, and like a man
haunted by fearful sights, became all at once
quite calm, and he said in a deep strong voice
which all the people could hear even over the
roaring of the sea, "I am an Hebrew, and
I serve the God of heaven, which hath made
the sea and the dry land." Then he told them
too why he had come with them, that he was
a prophet of this true and only God, and that
God had sent him on a work which he was not
willing to do, and that he had been so mad as
to think that he could fly from God, by crossing
over the sea; but that he had found he never
could fly from God: that in the calm God had
been with him, by night in the ship's sides, by
day on the deep. When the sun rose red in the
morning, when it burnt bright at noon, when it
set in the sullen sea at night, ever God was with
him, and he could not fly from His presence;
and now, that He had sent this storm, he doubted
not, as His messenger of wrath.

Then the men looked upon him with fear: and they asked him how he could have brought this trouble on them by his sin, and what they were to do with him.

Then he spoke again as calmly and as quietly as before, and he told them to take him up and cast him into the boiling sea. The sailors looked at him and trembled; and they did not dare to do it: so they rowed with great oars, and tried to guide and save the ship; but it could not be. The waves only grew larger and larger, and the wind higher and higher; and still the strange prophet said to them, " If you would have the sea become calm, cast me into its floods." Then at last the men thought they must do according to his word. So they prayed to God not to hold them guilty of this stranger's blood, if according to his own command they cast him forth into the sea.

Then they laid hold on him. It was strange to see him, who while he was flying from God was frightened at the very air, and started at every sound, now calm, and quiet, and fearless, though he was about to be cast into that terrible boiling sea. But now he was not afraid, because he dared look up again to his God.

So they cast him into the sea, and its great waves closed over him, and they saw him no more; and the sea became calm, and the vessel righted and went on her way peacefully.

But God had prepared a great fish which swam under those fearful waves, and when the prophet sunk under the waters, the fish swallowed him down. There was the prophet alive within the fish, who dived down to the bottom of the great sea and swam through all its storms, diving down lower than the roots of the mountains, amongst thick forests of sea-weeds, green, and red, and blue, which man's eyes never saw or shall see.

Then the prophet prayed unto his God. It was a strange place for prayer to come from; but faithful prayer can pass to God from anywhere; and from the fish's belly at the bottom of the deep sea, Jonah's prayer rose up to God on high. Then God commanded the fish, and he swam towards the shore of Jonah's country, and cast Jonah upon the shore. Strange and wonderful must have been his feelings when he stood once more upon the land; felt it firm under his feet, and looked out upon trees, and rocks, and houses, and faces which he had known before; for he was like a man who had come back to them from the grave and death. But one lesson surely he had learned, and that was, that man could not fly from God; for that earth, and sea, and air were full of Him, and did His bidding alway.

VI

THE TWO ROADS. A DREAM

[St Matthew vii 13, 14]

I HAD been reading in the New Testament before I fell asleep, and the words I had read came back again to me in a dream.

I thought I stood upon the edge of a wide common, and that from every side people were crossing the common by many different paths, to a place where they all met just by my right hand. There were already a great number of people there when I first looked, and more and more kept coming there continually. They were of all sorts and ages, rich and poor, young and old, sickly and strong; and I wondered, in my dream, what it was that brought them all together there.

Then I thought that I walked into the middle of the crowd, to see what they were about, and there I soon found what they were doing. I found that all the paths in which they had been walking, ended here in two different gates, and they were all doubting into which of these

two gates they should enter;—so I looked at the
gates with the rest, and cast my eyes down the
paths which lay beyond them.

A great many people were going in at the
first gate at which I looked, and I could not
wonder that they were. It stood wide open, and
seemed to bid all who chose to pass through it.
And then the path upon which it opened looked
as gay and pleasant as a path could look. There
was a bright gravel walk for those who liked it,
running between beds of beautiful flowers; and
a little on one side there was a smooth grass
walk which ran amongst fine spreading trees,
from whose green branches I thought every bird
of the air was singing. There were benches
placed here and there under those trees, where
every one could sit when he was tired, and rich
ripe fruits seemed to grow close by for them to
eat, and cool streams of water ran sparkling by,
so that no one need be thirsty who could stoop
down and drink. Then every one at first sight
looked so cheerful and happy along the way.
There were men and women singing and dancing,
and there were children gathering flowers, and
bright birds with silver feathers and golden eyes
flew round and round; and the trees were all
in flower, so that the air was quite scented
with their smell, and bees hummed amongst the

flowers, and the sun shone, and the rivulets danced, and all seemed alive and happy. I could not wonder for a moment that so many turned down this way.

Then I looked at the other gate, it was as narrow as the other was wide. It seemed indeed hardly wide enough to let any one pass, and so many found it. For I saw several who walked boldly up to it and began to push in at it, but it caught the clothes of one, and the flesh of another, and the bundle of a third, and they could not get through. I saw too sometimes a mother with a child in her arms, and it seemed she could not get through because of this child; and sometimes a father would hold a son's hand so fast, that neither could get in. What made this the stranger was, that in spite of its narrowness, every one was able to push in who tried with all their might. There were some very large people who pressed in, whilst others who were only half their size were kept out. Sometimes a mother, after much study, would be willing to let go her child rather than be kept without, and then it seemed to widen for them both, and they got in together. In a word, it seemed wide enough to let the largest in with a struggle, and too narrow to let any in without; though children got in the easiest, and those who had fewest things

to carry with them.   Few bundles, indeed, were
got in at all.

Nor were the troubles over when they had got
by; the path was almost as narrow as the gate.

Instead of the smooth walks, and gay flowers,
and the bright sunshine of the other road, here
the way was rough, and the tearing thorns grew
very close to each side of the path; and there
were many places in which it seemed to get
altogether dark, so that no one would be able
to keep clear of the thorns on one side or the
other.

When I saw all this, I wondered that any
should try to enter into it, instead of all hurrying
together down the gay and easy road.

But as I cast up my eyes, in my surprise
I saw that there was a motto written over each,
and I hastened to read them.   That over the
gate I was looking at said thus:

> The narrow path and thorny way
> Leads pilgrims to eternal day.

And then casting my eyes upon the other,
I read—

> This flowery way which men desire,
> Must end in everlasting fire.

Now when I had read these two mottoes, as
I knew that the KING who had put them up was

truth itself, I began to wonder how any could dare to go along the broad and easy way, though it did look so tempting; and I stopped to watch how it was that any dared to do so.

The first I saw was a fine high-spirited young lad, who, when I first looked at him, was still holding his father's hand. The old man looked somewhat sad, and I could see that he was struggling hard to get himself and his son up to the narrow gate. Just then there came by a party of merry young people, and they stretched out their gay hands to the poor boy, and looked into his face with their laughing eyes, and he slipped away from his father, and made with them towards the broad way. Just before he turned in, he looked round and said to his father, "I shall only go a little way with them, just to see what it is like, and then I shall turn back and follow you"; and then he passed into the green walk, and I could see him for a long way laughing and merry: but he never seemed to turn round again, and I never saw him come back.

And as I looked, I saw many more turning in the same way; some because they could not get a bag of money through the narrow way, and could not bear to leave it; some because they were afraid of tearing their fine clothes in squeezing through; some because it looked so dreary all down the narrow way, and they longed to gather the flowers and the fruits with which the broad way was full; some from mere thoughtlessness, and some because those who were round them began to jeer at them as soon as they turned their eyes towards the narrow gate. Some, too, I saw who went in at the broad gate, because, after walking a little way in the narrow road, they had got torn by the thorns which grew beside it. These seemed the saddest of any: they were always persuading every one to go in at the wide gate. "Trust us," they would say, showing the scratches upon their hands and cheeks, "trust us and be warned, for the path gets narrower and narrower, and darker and darker; and if you are fools enough to enter, you will soon wish yourselves out as we did."

Now hearing this said by one and another made me look a little closer at this narrow way. Then I saw that those who set out on it found mostly a few paces of easy walking just when they had squeezed through, and then that the path did get very narrow.

I heard one and another groan when the thorns tore his flesh, and there was hardly any one whom they did not tear sometimes. Those

45

who got in young, as they passed the most easily
through the gate, so they seemed to be getting
on the best now they were in, and generally
I could see that they who pressed on most
earnestly found the way the easiest, and got the
fewest rubs. But if any one began to loiter or
to look back, he was in the thorns in a moment;
and once in, no one could tell when they would
get clear; for first they were torn on this side,
and then on that; and even when they did get
clear, they always seemed to enter on one of
those dark places of the road through which they
went sighing, and groaning, and stumbling, like
men in a sore trouble and distress.

Many were so frightened by all this, that
they turned straight back, and fled towards the
narrow wicket, which then opened wide, and let
them out too easily.

Now I had a great curiosity to see how these
roads went on; and as I watched the walk in
the narrow road, I saw first that those who got
on quickly were often looking down to a book
which they held in their hands, and then again
looking up, as if to the heaven over their head.
When first I saw one of them look down, I
thought he would surely miss the track, and be
in a moment in the thorns; but instead of this,
it seemed as if he thus kept on straighter and

46

quicker than ever : while I was musing upon this,
I heard one of them read out of his book, " Thy
word is a light unto my feet, and a lamp unto
my path." And another seemed to answer him
at the moment by reading out—" Through Thy
commandments I get understanding, therefore
I hate every evil way." I saw, too, that instead
of the way getting narrower, and more rough
and thorny, it grew always easier, and smoother,
and broader. To those who had come in young,
it was very soon plain and pleasant ; and though
to the others it was longer rough, and they came
here and there to a fresh set of thorns, yet it
was plain that they got along much more easily
than they had done. Some who had been always
in the thorns on the one side or the other, were
now walking steadily along ; and some seemed
almost flying, they moved so quickly by, and so
easily. Flowers, too, began to blossom round
them ; the thorns turned often into sweet bunches
of roses and woodbine ; clusters, too, of ripe
grapes, of which they eat just enough to refresh
their lips, hung here and there in their way ; and
the birds began to sing sweetly to them.

No one now talked of turning back, but busy
as they seemed in pressing on, I thought they
looked already happy ; some, indeed, were joyous,
and all were cheerful ; and I overheard one and

47

another sing cheerily, "Her ways are ways of pleasantness, and all her paths are peace."

And now I could see, but a little way before them, a bright and cheerful light which shone upon their road. As one and another entered into it, I lost sight of them: but I could hear by their last words which reached me, that they were then happier than ever. Some were singing holy songs, as if to the sound of harps and music of all kinds; some were nearly silent, but the little they did sing came from hearts full of joy; and I doubted not that what I could not see beyond, was even happier and better than that I had seen.

I could scarcely bear to turn away my eyes from these happy people, to look at those who had chosen the other path: and when I did so, I was soon full of sorrow. For when I came to look more closely, I saw that even at the first, where they looked the merriest, there was hardly one amongst them who was thoroughly happy. The mirth, too, which they had, died away as they went further. If one stooped to gather the fruit or the flowers, they faded away as soon as he had them in his hand, or turned into dust and ashes as soon as they reached his lips. The saddest of all were those who had once set out along the other road; they were

48

ever turning round as if something affrighted them, or else pushing on madly as if they were running away from thought; and I could see, on looking closely, that the thorns still stuck in them and festered, and pricked them afresh at almost every turn. But though these were the saddest, yet as they went on all grew sad. Gloom and darkness came over those faces which had been the merriest. They were also ever falling out with one another, and so making matters worse.

When I saw them all so sad, I wondered that none thought of turning back and trying the other road. I soon found out a cause for this; for just as I was looking, I saw one try to turn; and lo, though he had been walking well and easily the other way, now I saw that he could scarcely stand. His feet slipped, his knees trembled, and he seemed all at once as weak as a young child: soon he slipped quite down; and as he lay bruised and groaning on the ground, those round him mocked and jeered at him! and I thought he would have risen no more— when, lifting his eyes up to heaven, he seemed to call for help, and then just scrambling up on his hands and knees, he got a few steps further, only to fall again, and groan again for help. At last, however, his feet steadied, and I saw him after many hard struggles reach the gate and push through it in spite of the crowd of people, who were thronging in and would scarce let him pass ; and he fled to the narrow gate and pressed through it, and went on along the path, though its thorns seemed to tear him at every step, and the way was darker than I had ever seen it yet : but still he pressed on like a man flying for his life; and I never took my eyes off him till at last he got into the easier and lightsome stage of his new journey.

But for the rest who did not turn, it was a heart-breaking thing to look at them. For sooner or later they all got into a thick black darkness, which was now spread all over what had once been their gay and cheerful road; and then I could see that they were parted from their friends, though they were most afraid of being alone; and then I knew that some worse thing befel them; for though I saw them not, I heard their cries and screams. They were exceeding loud and bitter, but they brought them no help, for they cried when there was none to hear; but they were so loud and bitter that I thought I could not bear to hear them; and so in my trouble I woke, and behold it was a dream.

VII

THE SPRING MORNING

IN a fresh and beautiful garden, full of every gay and sweet-smelling flower, I saw a merry party at play. Four boys made up the group; they were all of nearly the same size and age, and their light hearts laughed in their glad eyes, as they ran here and there in their sports and frolics. The very birds in the trees over them scarcely seemed happier than they—now chasing one another amongst the shrubs—now following some gay butterfly which floated by them on its blue and golden wings—now sitting by a murmuring stream which ran through the bottom of the garden, or refreshing themselves with wood strawberries, whose ripe red berries shone upon its banks.

Whilst I was watching their sports, delighted with their gaiety, I saw the figure of a man coming to them from amongst the trees which bordered the garden. He went and sat down in the shade, called the boys round him, and began to speak to them. There was something most kind and tender in this man's face and voice, grave though it was; and as he spoke, I could see that one or two of the boys looked very steadily at him, as if they wanted to catch every word that he said. None of them seemed careless, but one looked as if his spirit would come out through his eyes, so did he fix them on that grave kind face.

Then I thought that I drew near to the group, for they were not disturbed by my coming, and I listened to the words which were spoken to the boys.

"This," I hear the man saying as I came near, "this is the garden I have told you of. It is, as you see, a very gay pretty place, and one that you boys can be very happy in for a few hours' play. But it is not a place that you can stay in. All its pleasant sights would soon turn into terrors. The flowers would wither round you: one by one the birds would cease to sing. Your happy spirits would go—you would try to keep up your play, but it would grow into a business—all the sweet fruits would become bitter to your taste—the water of the stream would lose its freshness—you would alter too— and then, as you lost your pleasure in play, you would begin to tease one another and be un- happy: and then, worst of all, when the sun began to set, you would hear the roaring of many wild beasts all around you; as it grew darker you would see their fierce eyes glaring out of the bushes, from which now the sweet birds sing to you; and whilst you were trembling with fear, some of them would spring upon you and devour you.

"So that though this is a beautiful garden for an hour's play in the morning, it is not your home, and you must not try to make it so. Your home, as I have told you, is not very far before you. Between this garden and it there lies a waste and dreary-looking space, with some steep hills to climb; some hot places to pass; some slippery ways to walk over; but there is nothing to harm you if you follow my directions. I have myself passed over it, and you may trace my footmarks all along the way—the deepest always, and the plainest, where there is any trouble or danger: and when you have passed this plain and reached your home, then you may indeed be happy. For there are gardens sweeter far than this: there the birds make a never-ceasing music: there darkness never puts out the light: there are no evil beasts to harm you: there none are ever tired: but you shall always be happy; for all that are there love one another, and have all given to them that their hearts can desire."

THE SPRING MORNING

Then I saw that the eyes of the little boy who was listening so eagerly, sparkled brighter than ever, and a sweet smile came over his countenance, as he thought of that happy place. Then a happy grave look followed the smile, and I heard him say to the man, as tears filled his eyes, "And shall I see in that beautiful garden, my father, and my mother, and my sister, who are gone before me?" "Yes," said the man, looking kindly into the child's face, "if you reach that garden safely, there you will see them again, and nothing can ever part you more."

"But now," he went on, "hear how you are to reach it: first, take care and lose no time in setting out for it. Though this garden is beautiful and sweet, and the way you have to go is barren and steep, yet do not stay here, but set out at once. It is much easier to pass that road in the early morning. Even if you wait to the middle of the day it will grow harder, for then the sun will be hot, and the fresh dew will have dried off the green grass, and the hills will seem steeper to climb, and then perhaps you will grow weary, and halt till evening, and then it is dangerous; and the storms may gather, and the brooks you have to cross may swell; and if night should overtake you, you are lost. Then you would surely lose the foot-track, and either the miry

places would swallow you up, or the fierce beasts
that haunt that country would break out upon
you, and you would certainly be devoured by
some of them.

"This, then, is my first direction: Set out
at once, for the road is surest and safest in the
morning; and for the next, here are two gifts to
help you on your journey. Here is a reed-flute;
it is a small thing to look at, but do not despise
it, for it will be of great help to you. If you see
any of the wild beasts of the plain prowling
about, and sometimes they will venture out even
in the day, play a few notes upon it, and they
will surely leave you; or if you doubt about your
way, play upon it, and the foot-track will come
out again clear before your eyes; or if you are so
weary that you are ready to forget the beautiful
garden and rest at the end, play upon this, and
the thought of the end will come fresh again
upon your mind, and make you able to bear
the toil." So he gave each one of them a little
reed-flute, which he called "Prayer," and showed
them how to play upon it. Now they were com-
mon-looking flutes, but when they were touched
by the breath, methought the music they sent
forth was most sweet and piercing. When the
little Agapè[1] especially (for that was the name

[1] "Agapè" means "love."

55

of the boy who had asked whether he should see his father and his mother in the garden)—when Agapè put his to his lips, it sent out notes sweeter than the nightingale's. Then the man gave them each a small bottle full of what looked like the clearest water, and he said, "If you are at any time greatly weary with the way, take out this bottle and drink a few drops of its living water, and you will again be fresh and hearty. And now," he said, "farewell: I shall meet again in the happy garden all those who get there safely"; and so saying, he rose up, and walked slowly away from them until he was lost among the shadow of the trees from which he had come out.

Then I saw the little boys sit still for a while, as if they were thinking over the words that he had spoken; their echo seemed still to be speaking to them in the silence, and no one liked to be the first to disturb it. At last one of them, named Edonè[1], began: "Well, what do you say? of course we must all get away from this place before long, but I should like to have a little more play in it first."

"So should I," said Argia[2], "and to sit a little longer on this hill, and eat a few more

---

[1] "Pleasure."   [2] "Indolence."

of these refreshing strawberries before we set out on the long tiring journey. What say you, Astathes [1]?"

" I hardly know what to say; you see, we were so much advised to set out directly."

" Yes," added Edonè; " I do not mean to be late, but there can be no use in being in such a great hurry. It is quite morning now; if we were to play for another hour, and then rest a little, we should still be early; and I do not believe the sun will be any hotter then, and perhaps it will cloud over, or the wind will get up, and then, you know, it will be cooler instead of hotter."

" So it may, indeed," replied Astathes, " and I do not know why we should be in a hurry; but what do you say, Agapè?"

" That I mean to set out directly; and so I hope you will too. Think how happy we should be to get to that beautiful home early; and then, remember how we were told, more than once, that the earlier we set out, the easier it would be to us to travel; and I should have no pleasure in playing here, for thinking that the time was getting on, and that I had all my journey to go."

" I believe you are right," said Astathes; " so

[1] " Waverer."

57

if you are for setting out directly, I think I shall go with you."

"Well, then," said the other, "let us be off directly, for every minute seems long to me now." So he took his reed-flute, and hung his clear bottle at his side, and set out, and Astathes with him, for the side of the garden towards the plain. Then Edonè and Argia began to laugh at them, and say, "What a hurry you are in; we shall be there as soon as you, and have all the pleasure of playing here too."

Then Astathes halted a little, and seemed ready to sit down again; but Agapè took him by the hand, and away they began to walk. But Edonè grew angry at their going, and changed from laughing to scolding; and then seeing they minded not that either, he took up stones, and began to throw at them. Astathes was for stopping again to speak with him, but Agapè took his hand again, and said, "See, the sun is getting high over the hills even now; let us push on, soon we shall be out of the reach of his stones." But seeing Astathes still frightened, he said, "Let us try if the flute will help us"; so he played two or three notes of sweet music, and it seemed that, directly, they had got out of reach of the stones, and heard no more of the bad language which had troubled them.

So they walked on together, and began talking as little boys might talk. "Oh, Agapè," said Astathes, "I wonder how long the journey will take us! I long to get safely to its end."

"I hardly dare think yet of its end," said the other, "for we have only just set out; but I, too, long to get to the end."

"What a fine place that garden must be!"

"Yes, and there I shall see again my father and mother, and the kind sister who used to nurse me when I was little; and there we shall see the king of the country, who is kind to children, and loves to have them come and live with him."

So they talked, and now they had come nearly to the waste, and first looked out into it.

"It looks very dreary and rough, Agapè," said he.

"Oh! never mind its looking rough; I can see already a pathway through the thorns which frighten you."

"Well, if you were not with me, I think even now I should turn back."

"Never speak of turning back," said Agapè, and just then he reached the last stile which parted the garden from the waste. Lightly he sprang over it, and was setting out on the waste without thinking of looking behind, when he

59

heard the voice of Astathes, who had not yet crossed the stile.

"Wait a minute, Agapè; I want to gather some of this fruit to take with us; we shall have none, I can see, on the waste."

"No, no, dear Astathes, do not stop for the fruit; we shall find what we want on the way."

"But it looks so very barren."

"See, here is a good path; do not stop any longer, or I must go without you."

"Well, I will only gather a few more bunches of this fruit, and then I shall overtake you."

Agapè walked on a little, and then hearing Astathes call, he stopped again to speak to him.

"Why, how fast you get on! I am afraid I shall never keep up with you. I think I shall just stop behind, and come after you with Argia and Edonè; you know they are only staying a little behind."

Once more Agapè begged him to come, and once he almost persuaded him; he climbed half up the stile, but then he let himself down again the wrong side, and then he stood leaning against it, and gazing at Agapè, who was already almost out of sight over the first hill. So he stood for a time, and then when he could see no more of Agapè, and could hear nothing of the others, the stillness of the place began to frighten him;

and so after a while he stole back again to Edonè and Argia, who were still sitting on the pleasant bank, eating strawberries.

"So, here is one coming back again!" cried Edonè, who was the first to see him; and he began to laugh at him for the hurry in which he set off. Soon, however, they were good friends again; only Astathes would not join in laughing at Agapè, for in his heart he wished now that he had held on with him.

Then they thought that they would begin again to play together for a while, as they had done at first; but whether it was that the sun had got higher, and the air was too hot for play, or whether it was that the going away of Agapè had made them all dull, I know not, but they never were able to play as they had done. They were loud, but they were not merry; and as the sun rose higher and higher, they grew more and more tired of play and of one another. Then they sat down upon the bank to refresh themselves with the strawberries; but they had got hot too, and there was no refreshment in them; and Astathes began to think of what the kind grave man had said to them, and to wish in his heart more and more that he had gone with Agapè. So as these thoughts passed through his mind, he said to his two companions, "Had we not

61

better be thinking about setting off?" He spoke
as if he was half afraid to say it, and Argia
sleepily answered, "Why, the sun is just at the
hottest now! surely you would not think of going
now; we shall all be burned up with its heat."
But Edonè looked angry, and said quite crossly,
"I wish you had taken yourself off with that
fool Agapè, and not stayed here to tease us
about going."

"I am sure I wish I had," he answered sadly
enough; at which Edonè got quite into a passion,
and declared he should not stay with them any
longer, for that he spoiled all their pleasure; so
they drove him away, and he wandered very
sadly along the path in which he had set out
with Agapè, till he came to the stile leading to
the waste. Over this he looked out, and it seemed
more barren and thorny than ever; the sun was
very hot, and there was not a breath of wind;
and all up the hill-side there was nothing to give
him the least shelter; and the pathway by which
Agapè had gone in the morning seemed narrower
than ever, so that sometimes he could not see
it at all, but all looked like a wall of thorns,
through which he never could make his way;
and as he looked out, he wept, for his heart sunk
down within him.

But where, all this time, was Agapè? He had

felt lonely enough when first Astathes had stayed
behind; and as he climbed the first hill, he felt
its steep steps heavy travelling: he felt, too, that
he was quite alone, and that he was but a weak
child after all; so finding his heart beginning to
faint, he pulled out his sweet-voiced flute to help
his flagging steps, and played some sweet music
upon it; and, as he played, it seemed as if
heavenly words went along with the music, and
they said: "In the waste howling wilderness He
compassed him about." Then he thought of the
king, and his heart was lifted up, and straightway
he was at the top of the hill.

Now his path lay for a while downhill; and he
stepped on cheerfully and easily, until he came
into a low green bottom. Here a stream ran
across his path. He could see that sometimes
after rain it was swelled very high, and there
were marks put to show the traveller who should
come by at such seasons, how he might pass
without being swept away. But it was low now,
and there was no danger, so Agapè stepped
easily over the stones that were laid in it, and
gained the other side. Now as he pushed on,
the sun grew higher and higher in the heavens,
and Agapè began to feel faint and weary; then
he saw a soft green bank, and two or three
bushes threw a pleasant shade upon it, and he

63

was tempted to sit down upon it and sleep awhile; but as he drew near it, looking carefully, he saw a snake lying in the grass, which startled him; so then he remembered himself, and he saw that the deep footsteps of his guide had passed that bank by, and he thought, "Perhaps, if I had fallen asleep there, I had never waked again. No, I will push on to my journey's end—rest, rest, in the beautiful garden." But as the sun still scorched him, he thought of the bottle, and drawing it out he took two or three drops from it, and as he drunk, his ears seemed to be filled with these kind words: "The sun shall not smite thee by day, neither the moon by night." So he looked up, and saw just before him a grove of tall trees, and that his road lay under them. Right glad was he of their shelter, and of the breeze which blew gently through them, waving their high tops, and fanning his hot brow with its fresh breath. Now he made way easily and swiftly; and as he walked along, he could look around him into the wood, and, as he looked, he saw that on all sides of his path there were snares, and gins, and pitfalls, and sometimes the ground was all tumbled and torn by the mouth of the pitfalls, as if some one had fallen in and struggled mightily at the mouth to save himself; and once or twice

he saw in the gins and snares what looked like
the whitened bones of travellers who had been
caught in them. Then was he more thankful
than ever that he had passed through this wood
before it was nightfall, for "How," he said to
himself, "if it was but twilight—how should
I possibly escape these dangers?" With such
thoughts he passed along; and now, when he
was nearly out of the wood, he saw something
creeping on towards him from the left hand of
the path. He kept his eyes watchfully fixed upon
it, for fear of any evil, for he was a watchful
child: soon he saw that it was indeed a very
fearful beast, and in another moment he knew
that it was a great lion; already he could see
that the lion's eye was upon him, and his long
white teeth were gnashing, and he was just ready
to spring upon him. Then for a moment the boy's
heart sunk quite low, and he was ready to give
all over for lost, when the thought of his flute
came into his mind, and taking it quickly out of
his bosom he played a few earnest notes upon it.
As soon as the notes of the flute were heard,
the lion turned round and dashed away into the
thicket; and Agapè saw him no more, but instead
of his loud angry growl, it seemed as if the
refreshing breeze in the tree-tops formed itself
into words, and it said to him, "Watch and pray,

that ye enter not into temptation." "Resist the Devil, and he shall flee from you."

Then Agapè passed out of the wood, and as he came out of it, he could see before him in the distance, for the first time, the gate of the beautiful gardens, golden and shining; and within he thought he could see some heavenly figures, and he fancied that perhaps they were his sister, and his father, and his mother, looking out upon his weary steps as he journeyed over the waste. His heart yearned after them, but his feet were weary, and the sun smote upon his head, and it seemed the hotter for the pleasant shade which he had left. Then, as he was tempted to turn back again to the wood, he saw plainly marked upon the road the beloved footprints; and forthwith taking courage, he drew out his flute and played, and so pressed more cheerfully along the road. He had not travelled far, when he saw by the road-side a pleasant arbour; and though the footsteps had passed it by, he saw it written up in the writing of the king, that here it was lawful for weary travellers to rest awhile. So being footsore and worn, here he sat him down and drew out his bottle, and refreshed himself with its living water. Then as he sat, the heavens clouded over, and a mighty storm swept by; the rain fell in torrents, and he could hear the wild

66

beasts in the wood that he had left roar and moan, but they came not near him; and after awhile the storm passed over, the sky cleared again over head, and he set out on his way. The sun was now past its mid-height, and there was a pleasant air beating on his brow. So Agapè moved on speedily, and by the rate at which he was going, it would not be long before he reached the golden gates of the happy gardens.

But where all this while was Astathes, whom we left looking over the stile into the waste that lay towards the garden? Long did he stand there bewailing his folly that he had not gone with Agapè, until at last, looking up into the sky, he saw that the sun was past midday, and he thought how soon it would hasten to set, and therefore that he must at once begin his journey, unless he would give up all hopes. So, gathering all his courage, he sprang over the stile. But he had almost turned back again as soon as he had set out, so sorely was he pricked by the thorns. Either the way was really narrower than it had been in the morning, or he did not tread so steadily as Agapè: for where he had almost run, Astathes could now scarcely creep. A little, however, he did get on, though with many a rub and tear, and his feet and ankles were bleeding and wounded. Now, too, the path began to rise up the steep, and the sun was striking so hot upon his back that he was ready to faint. Then he thought of his bottle, and he drew it out ; but it had been corked so long, that the cork had got fixed so firmly in, it was long before he could stir it, or get the least drop from it. At last, however, he did, and [the words] "afterwards he repented and went" seemed to come with a promise of acceptance upon his spirit. And now he had not yet reached the top of the hill, when the storm that overtook Agapè safe in the king's arbour, fell upon him on the bare hill-side. Heavily did it beat upon him, as the rain fell in torrents, and the fierce gusts of the whirlwind swept by him, and the pealing thunder-clouds seemed to come quite down all around him. The ground, too, under his feet became miry with the rain, so that he fell back almost as much as he gained, and often slipped quite down into the dirt, bruising and wounding himself sorely. At last, however, he reached the top, and down the other side of the slope he got on something better ; though there, too, he slipped about, and got more than one shrewd fall. But when he came to the bottom of the slope, sorely was he put to it. The stream over which Agapè had passed so easily in the morning was now swelled into a roaring torrent, and it dashed along, foam-

68

ing, and boiling, and eddying, carrying all along in its course.

Poor Astathes! What shall he do? either he must venture into the stream, or he must give up for ever the rest of the happy garden. Just then he spied the posts which were set to guard travellers in the time of floods. So plucking up a little courage, he began to creep along by them. First, the water was ankle-deep, then it got knee-deep, then it rushed by his waist, and still the boy kept on, holding by the posts; another step, and it covered his shoulders, and lifted his feet from the ground; firmly he held on to the post, or he had been quite swept away by the stream, and carried down with it and drowned. When at last he gained his feet again, he knew not what to do. He was not nearly through the stream, and what if the next step he took he should lose footing of the bottom altogether, and the waters should pass over him, and he should perish? Then, first, he thought of his flute, and he said within himself, "Perchance this may help me." With sore trouble he drew it out, and tried to make some music upon it; but not a note could he sound. Then he saw that either in his many falls as he came along, or else whilst he was playing idly in the garden, the earth had got into his flute and almost

69

stopped up its small holes, so that no sound could pass. Here, however, the waters helped him, and by the time that he was almost benumbed, he had got the flute clear enough to be able to waken on it a few poor notes; and so soon as its sound was heard, the waters began to sink, and the child thought that he heard a sweet voice amongst their roaring. He could hardly hear what it said, but he thought it was this: " When thou passest through the floods they shall not overflow thee." Then did he dare put forth his foot again to try another step, and he found that he was already at the deepest part; so clinging close to the posts, and much fearing still lest there should be any ugly holes before him into which he might fall and be lost, but still saying over to himself the words that he had heard, he crept through and climbed, faint and weary, up the other side. When he reached it, he sunk down upon the grass, so cold and numbed and tired was he; and there he might have laid till he died, if he had not thought upon his precious bottle, which soon so far revived him, that again he girded up his strength, and passed on towards the wood.

Just at this very time Agapè was reaching the golden gates; the sun had not quite set, but it hung just over the top of the far hills, and shot

a red golden brightness over everything. Rich
and beautiful did those gates shine out before the
glad eyes of happy Agapè. Now he could see
plainly multitudes of heavenly creatures passing
about within, wearing light as a garment, and
crowns that looked like living fire. At times,
too, he could hear bursts of ravishing music,
which the garden seemed always to be sending
up on high, and some few notes of which strayed
out even into the pathway of the plain.

And now he stood before the gate; full was
his heart of hope and fear—a pleasant happy
fear, as if too much joy lay close before him.
Now all the troubles of the way were over, and
as he looked back, it seemed but a little moment
since he had left the beautiful but deceiving
garden in the morning, and all his troubles
seemed light. The scorching of the sun he
remembered no more, the weary hill-side, the
gin-set forest, and the lion's paws, all these
seemed little now, and he only thought of them
to thank the king who had brought him so safely
through all. As he lifted up his eyes to do so,
they lighted upon a golden writing, which was
hung over the gate. So he read the writing,
and it was, " Knock, and it shall be opened."
Then did he indeed draw in a deep breath, as
one does before doing some great thing, and

knocked with all his force; and so as soon as
he knocked, the golden door began to open, and
the happy boy entered the garden.

What awaited him there it is not given me
to tell; but from the blessed sounds which fell
upon my ear as the gate rolled back, I may not
doubt that he was entirely happy, for it was as
if the sound of a sea of heavenly voices suddenly
swept by me.

Just as Agapè reached the golden door, Astathes was entering on the wood. As he turned
into it, he saw the sun sink below the far-off
hills. Twilight came fast on, and he soon found
it very hard to trace out the path, so thick were
the branches overhead, and so faint and feeble
the remaining light. More than once he was on
the very brink of a deep pitfall, and only saved
himself from falling in by catching at the bushes
which grew round its mouth. More than once,
too, did he get his foot entangled in those gins
and snares wherewith the side of the path was
full, and only escaped from them grazed and
hurt by the sharp teeth of the biting traps. On
all sides of him, too, wild beasts were roaring.
Now had that come true, of which in the morning
he had been warned, that out of every bush,
instead of the liquid notes of sweet singing birds,
there should gleam forth upon him the fiery eyes

of savage monsters thirsting for his blood. As
he heard their deep roars, or, more near to him,
the savage snapping of their sharp teeth—as he
saw their fiery eyes, and almost felt the brushing
of their soft or wiry hides, he felt more than
ever before how foolish he had been in losing
the morning-hours, and not passing through the
wood whilst the sun was high. His escaping all
these dangers was a wonder above the power of
man. But as he went into the wood, he had
taken his flute out of his bosom, and though he
could not draw from it such music as came from
the breath of Agapè on his, yet now, by care
and trouble, it was much freed from its earthly
hindrances, and made a low clear music. All
the wood through did Astathes keep playing on
the flute; never was it from his lips; and though
he woke from it no sounds of pleasure, or of
triumph, yet it doubtless saved him from the
fierce jaws which on every side were gaping for
him, and he passed out of the wood in safety.
But when he entered on the plains beyond, no
such clear sight of the golden gates or the
happy gardens gladdened his eyes as Agapè had
seen. Perchance in the twilight there was a little
brightness thereabouts, but it was dull and uncertain; and after his frights in the wood, the
boy's heart would have fainted wholly within him,

73

if it had not been for the precious bottle, with which he moistened his parched lips. "He shall make thy darkness to be light," the waving boughs of the trees then seemed to murmur to him, as he walked from under their shelter; and this raised his spirits, so that he again set forth. Now was he by the arbour, but the twilight was too far advanced for him to see it, or to rest therein. So, weary and distressed, he pressed forward, until at length a "light rose upon his darkness"; for he too, as he drew nearer to the golden gates, was soothed with some soft sounds of mercy, until, with a beating heart and a straining eye, he seized the golden knocker, and oh, joy of joys! the gate opened for his entrance, and Astathes, poor wavering Astathes himself, of the king's bounteous goodness, entered the heavenly garden.

But what, all this day through, were Edonè and Argia doing?

After they had driven Astathes from them, they sat for a while longer on the same grassy bank, dreamily doing nothing. Then as the sun grew hotter and hotter, Argia fell asleep, and Edonè strolled some way from him to gather the rich-looking ripe fruit which hung from a tree a little further on; there he sat for hours, eating the fruit, and throwing the stones playfully from

74

him, whilst Argia still slept on in the pleasant
shade, until the sun was beginning to set. Just
at that moment Edonè saw a fierce beast coming
nigh to Argia. He thought it very shocking to
see his friend eaten up by the beast, but he was
much more afraid for himself, and he thought
that if he called to wake up Argia, the beast
might perhaps turn upon him instead. So he
tried, without making any noise, to steal away
into the wood. The beast came up to Argia,
who slept so soundly that he seemed to be dead;
when just at that moment Edonè shook the
bushes as he fled away. The evil beast looked
up, and seeing Edonè, he sprang like lightning
after him, and Argia was first woke up by hearing the dreadful shrieks of Edonè, as the beast
seized him in his claws, and doubtless tore him
in pieces. It was a sad hearing for Argia. He
started up and ran he knew not whither; then
he thought of his flute, and felt for it in his
bosom, but it had fallen out whilst he slept, and
he hardly dared steal back to look for it. At
last, however, he did; but when he found it, it was
so bent and bruised in his sleep, that it seemed
as if it never again would make any music.
However, having found it, he started off as fast
as his feet would carry him; and as it happened,
he run straight to the stile over which Agapè and

75

Astathes had passed. In his sore fear he sprang over the stile, and began to hurry up the hill in spite of the thorns and the steepness. But there he was lost from my eyes in the gathering darkness of the night, and I know not how it fared with him further. Whether he was drowned in the swollen stream, or lost in the pitfalls, or snared in the gins, or devoured by beasts, or whether he did straighten and tune his marred flute, and with the help of its music just reach the golden gates, I cannot say; but I greatly fear for Argia, for I know who it is that hath said, "The night cometh when no man can work."

VIII

THE RUNNERS

[1 Corinthians ix 24—27; Heb. xii 1]

I DREAMED that I was walking through
a foreign country far away from this land, and
I thought I came to a wide grassy plain, sprinkled
over here and there with shrubs and trees, between which lay an open space, looking as green,
and smooth, and fresh as a newly-mown lawn;
and as I was casting my eyes over it, and
wondering why it was kept so smooth, I saw a
number of persons all crowded together at one
end of it; so I walked on till I joined them,
that I might learn what was going on. There
I saw several of the group dressed all alike,
and could soon see that they were ready to run
a race. They had cast off all those clothes which
could hinder them in running, and they seemed
to be all ready to set out as soon as the signal
should be given. While I was looking at them,
a herald of the king of the land came out of his
tent, and began to read to them the rules of the
race. He told them that the king would give

crowns to all that strove earnestly in that race;
that these crowns would be brighter than any
crowns of this earth; and that he would take
every one who won a crown, to receive him into
his family, and treat him as his own son; and that
such should never suffer more, or want anything;
but that they should dwell for ever in the king's
palace, and be as happy as heart could wish.
He told them, too, that all who halted in the
race, or did not run earnestly, would lose these
crowns, and that they would be as surely punished
as the rest would be rewarded; that they would
be cast into a dark and dreary country, where
they would work ever under hard taskmasters,
and groan for their stripes and misery, without
help and without hope.

When I heard these rules, I looked more
earnestly than before upon the men who were
about to run, and to my surprise I saw that
there were many more than I had seen at first.
There were many whom I had thought mere
bystanders or lookers-on, but who I now saw
were indeed amongst the runners. Yet I could
scarcely believe it. For they were not dressed
like the others; they had taken no care to gird
up their loins: some of them had long flowing
clothes, which must get in their way as soon as
they began to run; some were eating and drink-

ing, forgetting that they had a hard struggle
before them, and would need to be as light and
as active as possible when they got into the
race; and yet all seemed to think that they
should do very well, and made no doubt at all
that there were crowns for them as well as for
the rest.

Even amongst those who were better prepared, I could see, on looking closer, a great
difference between some and others. Some were
strong and active, and looked as if they could
not fail of getting the first crown, and living for
ever in the happy palace of the king; whilst
others were pale and faint, as if they had hardly
any strength to walk, and must fall short as soon
as they began to run. Some seemed too old to
do anything but hobble, and some so young that
they could scarcely do more than crawl.

Whilst I was looking them over and over,
and waiting eagerly to see the end, I heard
a trumpet sound, and all who were to run got
ready for the start. Soon another trumpet
sounded, and away they set. For a few paces
all went on together, but only for a few. First
I saw that those who had been carelessly eating
and drinking, and never thinking of the race
they had to run, began to flag and faint. One
after another they halted, and as the rest ran

79

on, they were soon left altogether behind. Then
I saw that one and another of those who would
not put on the runner's dress, began to stumble
and fall as their long clothes caught the wind
and entangled their feet. So they, too, were left
behind. Only one or two of them began to strive
to cast off their long garments, and to gird up
their loins like the better runners. But whilst
they stopped for this the rest passed on, and
they were left quite behind; all but one, who,
though he was a good way behind, yet seemed
determined not to lose the crown, and so laboured
mightily to regain the ground that he had lost,
and I could see him still following, though far
behind, and looking very weary and distressed,
but still pressing on as one who would not give
up the struggle.

And now their number was sadly thinned,
and I could look all the closer at those who still
followed on. One brave runner there was who
took the lead of all; he was made for speed and
strength, and though he was at the head of the
race, he did not seem to labour so much as many
that got on less quickly, for he often looked
round to see how others fared, and had a jest
ready when this one fell off, and a joke when
another stumbled. As they turned a corner in
the course, I heard one of the king's heralds

speak to this man in a grave sad voice as he went by, and he seemed to say to him: "Let him that thinketh he standeth, take heed lest he fall."

Then there followed another, and he too was a brave runner; he set his feet firmly on the ground, and drew his breath so evenly, it seemed as if nothing would weary him. But as I watched his running, I saw that he hardly ever looked on to the end of the course. He had his eyes sometimes on the ground, sometimes on those near him; and if a bird did but fly out of a bush with gayer feathers than the rest, or if the air was scented with sweet-smelling flowers, he would make a half-stop, as if he must stay for them, before he could go on with the race. A little way behind him came another, and he, too, me-thought, promised well for a crown, for he, too, had a strong step and an active body; but his eyes, too, were wandering, and once or twice I thought, as he passed near the fruit-trees of that land, on which grew fruit of gold and silver, that I saw him catch at the beautiful boughs, as if he wished to fill his hands even whilst he ran the race. I heard one of the heralds speak to these two also; and to the first he said, in a chiding tone, and yet full of kindness, "I press toward the mark"; and to the other, "Laying aside every weight"; but it did not seem to me that his words sunk much into their hearts. For a little while, indeed, they ran more steadily, but soon I could mark their eyes wandering, and their hands stretched out, just as they were before the warning.

Some way after these there came another. He was not so strong as those who had gone before, but there was a great firmness in his face, and his eyes seemed set straight on, as if he looked at something in the air before him. Then I strove more earnestly to see on what his eyes were set, and I could see far before him the end of the course, and there the judge's chair was set, and the judge himself was seated in it. He was a grave and comely person, and a crown was on his head, and at his right hand there were shining crowns stored up for those who prospered in the race; and I thought as I looked, that his eyes were on the steady runner, and that he looked at him with kindness and love.

Then came another, and he was nimble and light of foot, though he was now so far behind,— a little while before, and he had been the front of all; and then he had stopped to take breath, as though he were confident that at any time he could regain the ground that he had lost:

and so now he was far behind, and there came
a warning to him from one of the heralds, and
it was this, "Be not weary in well-doing," and
when he heard it he started forward, and got
nearly to the head of all; but then he grew
slothful, and began to pause again, as if the
race was nothing more than sport, and its bright
crown no better than a jest. While he was thus
loitering, I noticed one come up whom I had
marked at first as very lame and aged. He
had soon been left behind: yet still there was
a great earnestness in his countenance. Many
times when I thought he must have given in,
I heard him call upon the name of the king, as
if he would not be left behind, and then strength
came unto his weakness, and he got on nobly in
the course. Lame, too, as he was, I saw him
often lend a hand to a poor feeble-looking runner
who was pressing on behind him. He, too, was
in earnest, but he was very weak, and often his
steps tottered, and he caught at the hand of the
lame man, or he must have fallen; and so it
was, that whenever the lame man helped him
on, instead of being delayed by his kindness,
he seemed to help himself too; and the crown
looked brighter at the end of the course, and
the judge's chair and the goal seemed to come
nearer to him.

THE RUNNERS

Now behind them came a fair child, beautiful to look upon, and almost with the face of an angel; but how its little feet could bear the road, or what could put into its young heart to run the race, I could scarcely think, till I saw that a hand was guiding it I had not seen at first, and there was written upon it in letters of gold, "He shall gather the lambs in his arms": so then I knew that the little child was safe, and I fancied that I could see the judge holding out the crown which was to adorn that infant head.

But as I gazed, I heard a cry as of one in distress, and I looked round, and I saw the foremost runner fallen all along upon the ground. Alas, he had not minded the warning of the herald, he had not fixed his eyes upon the crowns and the goal; and so, as he was looking idly round to see how others fared, he stumbled and fell, and now he lay all along upon the ground, and he could not regain his footing. The ground where he had fallen was all miry and unsound, and the more he struggled the more he sunk into it. I heard him cry out, and a sharp sad cry it was; but I never heard him call upon the king, and so he lay struggling and labouring, until all had passed him by, and he was left behind.

The others passed on; but the careless runner, I grieved to see, was still running carelessly, and

looking no more towards the end of the race,
nor pressing more towards the mark, than when
I saw him last. I feared for him too; and even
as I looked, a beautiful bird of the rarest feathers
fluttered out of a bush by the side, and almost
within his reach. I saw his eyes sparkle, and he
turned a little on one side; it was only a little,
and he did not wholly cease from his running,
but that little cost the poor man his crown; for
there were secret spikes set amongst that grass
which lay out of the road, and as he hurried on
after the gay bird which fluttered just before
him, he trod amongst the spikes and fell; and as
I looked, I saw that it was written up, just where
he had left the smooth grass of the course, "The
way of transgressors is hard."

He who had been warned at the same time
by the king's faithful herald, was just by when
his companion turned aside out of the way; and
when he saw the other fall, for a time methought
it made his countenance graver, and he raised
his eyes and looked off from the trees of gold
to the far end of the course. And then there
fell a light upon his face, which I had never
seen on it before. But soon it died away, and
a film gathered over his eyes, and the crowns
and the end were hidden from them; and just
then a golden bough stretched quite out into

the middle of the road, and its fruit of silver and of gold almost touched his hands. He looked at it, and I feared that he was lost. He stopped to handle it. He gathered some of its rich fruit, and began to load himself with it. Just then came up the slower runner, whose eyes had ever been fixed upon the end. To him he offered some of the spoil, if he would stay and help to gather it; but the man could not take his eyes off from the end; and so he looked not round upon the baits with which the other strove to tempt him, but saying, "I press toward the mark," he was for passing on his way. The sound of those words which he had heard of old from the herald, startled the other somewhat, and he let the bough go. Then there came, as from the air, a voice which said, "They that will be rich fall into temptation and a snare"; and again, "But thou, O man of God, flee these things." When he heard these words, the faithful runner hastened on his way; and even the tarrying runner trembled and set out again upon his course. But he could not bring himself to cast away the fruit that he had gathered; and it grew heavier and heavier, as he strove to carry it, until first he halted, and then he fell by the wayside, pierced through with many sorrows.

THE RUNNERS

Then there passed by one running bravely, with his face towards the goal, and his steps nimble; and I was glad when I saw the man so earnest, for I could see that it was the same who had fallen back before, from loving to take his ease; and now I had good hopes for him, that he would hold on to the end. Yet even as he ran, my heart misgave me for him; and I looked round with more confidence on the lame man and his fainting friend, who were striving to reach the end. Close by them, too, was the fair child, who seemed to glide along the way, so easy was his running. I could not take my eyes from them, though I could hear still further back the voice of one calling on the king for aid, and I thought by the sound that it grew somewhat nearer. But as I listened to it, I heard a sound of the sweetest music, and I saw, on looking up, that it came from golden harps, on which men clothed in white were playing round the judge's chair; and now they touched their harps because one had reached the end. Then I drew near to see who was the happy man: it was not the man who had just before passed me so nimbly, but it was the slower runner whose face had been set so steadily to the end of the race. And I saw that as he drew near the king smiled upon him with a loving smile;

and he spake the word, and a crown was brought
to him, and he set it on his servant's head. It
was bright to look upon, like the diamond and
the topaz, and on it there was written, in letters
of fire which flashed out on every side, " Be thou
faithful unto death, and I will give thee the
crown of life."

Then the golden doors of the king's palace
were rolled back, and beautiful lights and sounds
were seen and heard from within, and I saw the
crowned runner walk towards the door, and he
passed within, and the happy crowd within
thronged about him, and gave him a glad welcome; and though I could but just see his face,
I saw that joy sat upon it, that the struggle of
his hard race was over, and that sorrow and
sighing had fled far away. Much did I long to
go in with him into the happy place, but it was
only for the runners; and the golden gates shut
soon upon him, and hid their joy from those
who were without.

Whilst I was wishing to run in the race
myself, I heard the harps of gold touched again,
and give out their sweet music. Then I looked
up, and three more of the runners drew near.
The lame man, and the fainting runner, and the
fair child, stood before the judge's chair. The
king looked on them with his mild love, and he

called straightway for crowns, which he set upon their heads. Then I saw that on the crown of the lame man it was written, "He that endureth to the end, the same shall be saved"; and turning to him who had so often almost fainted in the way, and who could even now scarcely believe that he was safely landed at the goal, I saw it written on his crown, "To him that hath no might, he increaseth strength"; whilst the fair child looked fairer and more beautiful than ever, and he bore upon his crown the writing, "Suffer the little children to come unto me, and forbid them not, for of such is the kingdom of heaven."

Then these three walked together towards the golden doors, which opened for them of their own accord, to the sound of the sweetest music; and they, too, went in and were soon mingled with the happy people there.

Then I thought within myself of the man who had passed so nimbly by me, and promised so well for a crown, and yet who had not reached the end. So I walked slowly down the course to see if I could light upon him. I had gone but a little way from the end when I saw a choice arbour, shady with flowery shrubs, and sweet with every scented flower, and there on the mossy seat within I saw the nimble runner stretched out at length, and fast asleep. So I tried to awaken him, but could not—he only turned in his sleep and slept the sounder. My heart was grieved for the man; but as I came out of the arbour, I saw he had not been unwarned, for it was written up over the doorway by which he had come in, "Slothfulness casteth into a deep sleep."

And as I came out I heard the same voice of one calling on the king which I had heard before, and looking round I saw the runner who had so late cast off his flowing robes, and girded himself for the race. He was toiling indeed with his eye fixed on the end, and yet only seeing its brightness at times; and when it was clouded over, I heard him call again upon the king, like one who feared that all was lost.

But now his troubles were well-nigh over, for soon he heard the welcoming music of those heavenly harps; and a crown was brought out for him which shone with these words, "Faint, yet pursuing"; and the golden door opened for him, and the scales fell altogether from his eyes, and all the labour of his race was forgotten in the fulness of the joy which flowed into his soul. So whilst I was thinking how I could myself begin to run in this race, I awoke, and behold it was a dream.

IX

THE YOUNG SHEPHERD

[1 Samuel xvii 34—37]

IN a large upper room, just under the flat roof of the house, sat a family at breakfast. They were round a rude wooden table, and they lay along on benches which were placed round its sides.

A fine family they were to look on, that old venerable man and his eight sons. The three who were the nearest to their father looked like soldiers. They belonged to the king's own guard, and proud enough they were that they did so. There were no finer men in all the camp of Saul than these, when they went out after him in their shining armour, treading strongly on the ground, and making it rattle and shake under their brazen greaves. Now they sat unarmed like the rest round the table, eating the loaves and parched corn and cheese and butter which their father had brought out of his stores, and the fresh honey in the honey-comb which their youngest brother had found in the wood.

The old man looked happily round upon his

sons, and perhaps his eye rested with an especial
love upon his youngest; for he was still a lad,
not come to the height or strength of his
brothers, and his long hair curled over his ruddy
countenance, which looked fresh and clear as the
dewy morning. A stranger would not much have
noticed him amongst these strong, fine men, his
elder brothers; and they all despised him for
his youth, and left him to take charge of their
father's sheep. But there was ONE who did not
despise him. There was ONE who looked on
him with far more favour than on those proud
and haughty soldiers, and that ONE was God.
For this young lad had sought and found the
God of his fathers. He was a holy youth—
he loved to hear of God—he knew all the
wonderful histories of his people of old, how
God had chosen Abraham, and blessed Isaac,
and preserved Jacob. He loved to hear of the
time when, in the far wilderness, Jacob had laid
his head upon a stone to sleep, and God had
sent him the beautiful visions of His holy angels
coming up and down as on a ladder from the
earth to heaven; on all these things he would
think and ponder as he sat watching the sheep
in the waste, and sometimes you might see his
hands clasped together in earnest prayer to this
great God of Abraham; sometimes his eyes

would fill with tears, which would run all down
his cheeks, as he thought of these deep things,
and longed to know God more himself, and to
see some of these wonderful and great sights
which holy men before now had seen. Sometimes
you might hear him playing on a little harp,
which he loved so well that he seldom went to
the far folds without it ; and then he would sing
to its music, and pour out the most holy and
heavenly praises and psalms. God was teaching
this shepherd all these holy songs, in which his
full pure heart ran over when he praised and
gave thanks unto His name.

Once when he was thus praising and thanking
his God, he did find in a wonderful way that God
was near unto him. It was the winter time ; the
snow lay upon the high grounds, and the wind
roared and howled through the woods, making
the tops of the cedar-trees bow and murmur like
the waves of the sea, or the whispering of some
great army in a place of many echoes. He had
pent up his flock in a sheltered place, under the
lee of a high wood, and as he sat watching them
and listening to the tossing trees, it seemed to
him as if the voice of the wind and the murmur
of the forest was a song of praise to the God of
all. "I will not be silent," he said within himself,
"whilst all things are praising the Lord"; so he

93

took up his harp, and began to sing to the wild notes which it flung forth as his hand swept over it. Perhaps he sang as he once did, " Praise the Lord upon earth; ye dragons and all deeps; fire and hail, snow and vapour, wind and storms, fulfilling His word; mountains and all hills; fruitful trees and all cedars; beasts and all cattle...young men and maidens; old men and children; praise the name of the Lord, for His name only is excellent, and His praise above heaven and earth."

Hardly had he finished the last words when he thought that he heard a roaring louder and nearer than that of the forest behind him, and looking up, he saw that a great lion and a savage bear, whom cold and hunger had brought from the mountain-woods into the plain, were coming near the fold that he was keeping.

It was a fearful sight to see those savage beasts drawing near to him. The lion crouching along the ground, its long tail stretched straight out behind it, its eyes fixed, and looking ready to spring upon him in a moment; the bear, too, with its heavy awkward trot, fierce red eyes, and shaggy head—this was a fearful sight to a lonely shepherd boy on a far hill-side. He might call as loud as he would, and no man would hear him or help him.

But was he frightened? These thoughts, you may be sure, came fast into his mind as he looked at the fierce and evil beasts; but he was not frightened, for other thoughts came with them. It came into his mind, as if God had sent the thought, that though no man was there, yet that he was not alone; that God was very nigh to him, and that never was he so little alone as when all men were afar off, and God was near him. So he lifted up his heart to God and said, "O Lord God of Abraham, be nigh unto Thy servant that prayeth"; and then with a great shout he rushed upon the beasts with no more than his shepherd's staff. And God was with him of a truth, and so mightily was he strengthened, that he seized the beasts by the beard, and slew them in the strength of the God of all.

Then he blessed and praised the Lord. But he made no vaunt of what he had done; only he stored the thought of it up in his heart; and many times afterward, when danger threatened him, he said within himself, "The Lord which delivered me out of the paw of the lion, and out of the paw of the bear, He will deliver me."

X

THE TENT ON THE PLAIN

"And he was baptized, he and all his, straight-way."—Acts xvi 33.

In my visions I saw a tent pitched upon a fair plain. It was a large tent, of the purest white cloth, so that it might be seen afar off; and when the sun shone brightly upon it, and the wind lifted up the folds of a great flag which hung from its top, it was indeed a noble sight. When the flag unfolded itself in the breeze, you might see upon it a blood-red cross, upon a ground of snow-white silk.

Many people were going in and out of the tent. Sometimes a single man would go in silently and thoughtfully, with a heavy countenance, and he would come out again after a time, with a glow upon his face, and a firmer step than that with which he went in. Sometimes a husband and wife would go in together; sometimes a father and a mother, with their children; sometimes a child would lead in an old man; sometimes a mother would pass in with an infant in her arms; some, too, would go in carelessly and lightly just because others did, and these seemed to come out pretty much as they went in; or if for a while they were graver, and seemed more earnest, it soon wore off again, and they were as light and thoughtless as ever.

While I was musing upon this strange sight, and wondering what it might mean, methought some one tapped lightly on my shoulder. I looked round, and there stood by me a comely person with a grave, kind air, but with eyes in which there was such a brightness, that when I looked into them I felt abashed, and fixed mine down upon the ground.

Whilst I cast about in my mind how I should speak to him, he first began, and said to me, in a mild voice which chased away my fears, "You would see the inside of this tent, and know what is doing in it? then follow me, and I will show you."

Thereupon he took me by the hand, and led me down to the tent door, which he lifted up, and we stood within. There were many people within, of all ages and countries, gathered round one who stood high above them all. He was clothed like the grave man who had brought me in, but was not so bright and terrible to look upon; his voice, too. was soft and winning, and when he turned to any, it was with a smile of kindness which drew their hearts after him, so that the very children in the tent came near, without their little hearts failing them, as one by one he called them to him.

Then my guide led me nigh to this man, and placed me at his side, that I might see and hear all that passed between him and those that were with him in the tent. Just then there came to him a man of middle years, with a sad, heavy countenance; his eyes were fixed on the ground, and I could see that salt tears were falling from them, and running over his hard, manly cheeks. Kindly and tenderly spake the man in white to him, and bid him fear not, for that he was about to serve a gracious master. The words seemed by their very sound to open the poor man's heart, for he looked up, and almost smiled amongst his tears. He said, too, something about having "fought long against the king, and served his enemies, and resisted his messages; and that he feared he should not now be received as a soldier." Then the man in white bid him look up, and whether it was a beautiful picture or a heavenly vision I know not, but he saw the forms of bright soldiers in golden arms, with crowns upon their heads, and happy faces, which seemed bathed in light, so gloriously did they shine; and one and another looked on the man kindly, and seemed to beckon him to join them, till his eyes began to sparkle and his heart to beat high with hope.

Then the man in white bid him look in upon himself; and when he saw how unlike he was to them, his heart began again to die away, but the man raised him up by saying to him, "And such were some of them; yea, all of them, like you, were rebels once." Then he told him how the king had provided for those that undertook his service, that they should always be held up so long as they looked to him for help, and that he would himself ever be near them; that though they could not see him with their eyes, or feel him with their hands, yet that he would be close by them, and that he would put strength into their arms, and cover them in the day of battle; that he himself would help them to be faithful to him, if they sought his help; and that then he would at last take them to dwell with him in his palace, where they would sit at his board, and hear his voice, and see his face for ever.

The poor man's eyes brightened at the sound of these brave words, and he said, "This is what I want indeed, but are you sure that the king will receive, as his soldier, one who has so often rebelled against his will and refused to serve him?"

"Of that I can make you sure," said the man in white; "here is the king's own hand and seal for what I do," and with that he opened a book which was sealed with the king's seal, and he read to him from it, "Go ye into all the world, and preach the gospel unto every creature; he that believeth and is baptized, shall be saved." And again he showed him in another place, "Him that cometh unto me, I will in no wise cast out"; and again to cheer his heart the more, he showed him this, "Your sins and your iniquities will I remember no more."

Then was the man's heart glad indeed, and with a cheerful voice he said, "Oh, sir, let me enter quickly into the service of the king." Then the man in white questioned him once more, whether he did indeed believe the king's word, and would fight his battles and strive against his enemies; and when he had heard his answer, firm and yet humble, he brought out a book, in which he wrote down his name as one of the king's soldiers; then he made upon his forehead the sign of the same cross which I had seen upon the banner, and told him that now he was one of the king's men, and that he must bear him true love unto his life's end. Then he called

him nigh unto himself, and he drew out from
the king's treasures a bright and beautiful ring,
which he put upon his finger, and called it the
ring of adoption. There was in it one stone,
which burnt and sparkled like living fire, and
round it was written as in flame—"Faith." As
he put it on his finger, he said to him, "Whilst
this ring remains on thy finger, thou art safe;
and whilst this stone burns and sparkles so
brightly, nothing can draw it off; but if ever
this grows dull, then look to the ring, for it will
begin to grow loose upon thy finger; and if it
once falls off, then thou art lost. And now go
thy way, and God speed thee." So I saw that
the man went his way with a glad and cheerful
countenance.

Then came another before him, and with him
he dealt in like manner, and so did he with his
wife, for she too was led to wish to do the king
service; and I heard him say to her, that some
of those whose crowns were brightest, had been
once but as she was now—a weak woman and
ready to fall.

So they were turning away, when the eyes
of the man in white fell upon a child which she
was leading by the hand, and a little infant
whom she was shielding in her bosom; so he
looked upon her again, and spoke and said, "And

will you not give up those little ones, too, to do the king's service?"

Then her eyes sparkled more brightly than ever, and she said, "Oh yes, sir, if I may; but how can such little ones perform any service to our king?"

Then the man in white answered her again, "It is true, even the eldest of them can scarcely serve him yet, that you can see; but the king is full of love, and he would fain have such little ones given up to him: and he will put their names in his book, and give them the ring of adoption, if their parents will bring them unto him, and promise in their names, that when they grow to years, they will serve their king; and then the king will trust them unto you, to bring them up for him. Look," he said, "here is the king's word for it." So he opened the sealed book again, and read from it, "Suffer the little children to come unto me, and forbid them not"; and again, "The promise is unto you and to your children." Then were the hearts of the parents glad, and thankfully did they promise for their children that they should serve the king here-after; and the sign of the cross was marked upon their foreheads, and their names were written down in the king's book, and the ring of adoption was put on their small fingers. Then the man

made them observe, that there was such virtue
in these rings, that though they fitted now the
smallness of these infant fingers, they would fit
them still hereafter, though they grew up to
man's estate and size. He showed them, too,
the stone of faith set in them; but in these little
rings it sparkled not outwardly. "Already,"
said he, "is there in these stones some inward
sparkling, though it cannot be seen outwardly;
but as the children grow in reason, if they grow,
too, in grace, the stones shall begin to sparkle
outwardly. Be it your care to draw out this
shining." Then I saw that the mother believed,
and so the stone in her own ring waxed brighter
and brighter; but for a moment it seemed to
me that the father doubted, and looking down
upon his ring, I saw that the stone in it was
cloudy. But even while I watched it, it was as
when a cloud clears off from the sun, and the
man looked up and thanked the king, who had
taken his little ones so soon into his good and
happy service. So they and their children passed
on and left the tent.

And I stood and saw others come before the
man; and some came as these had come, and
some seemed to come with lightness and no
thought. Then I saw that the man looked very
gravely upon such; and he told them that the

king whom they wished to serve was one who
" searched all hearts, and from whom no secrets
were hid." Then he questioned them closely,
and only if they still said that they desired to
serve the king, he wrote down their name, and
their children's, in the king's book of service,
and put the rings upon their fingers; but this
he did with a sorrowful face, and told them that
if they were not faithful to the king, it would
make him punish them more dreadfully than
others, that they had thus been called his servants,
and entered as soldiers under him.

For some time had I looked on this sight,
and marked many coming in and going out, until
I longed to know how it went with them after
they had left the tent—how they fought, and who
were faithful, and how the little ones grew up
who had been so early made soldiers of the king.
And as these things were in my mind, methought
my guide touched me again, and said, " Thou
wouldst see further the end of this matter? then
follow me." So I walked after him out of the
tent. Then my vision was changed; for it was
now the first dawning of a summer morning, and
we were crossing a mountain-side, until we stood
over a pleasant valley, green with fields, and
bright with many flowering trees, and gay flowers
growing in little gardens, round thatched cottages,

from the chimneys of one or two of which the grey-blue smoke was just rising, straight and still, into the clear morning air.

Then methought my guide cast on my shoulders a beautiful mantle, and straightway we stood within one of the cottages, unseen by those around us. We were in an upper room, which was clean and sweet; for the window was open in the thatched roof, and honeysuckle and sweet roses hung in bunches by it. There were two beds in the room, and one little cradle; and the clothes on the bed were very coarse and rough, and mended, but all clean and neat and white. In the cradle slept a beautiful babe, and as its little hands were crossed over its breast, I could see that it wore such a tiny ring as had been put upon the children in the tent. In one of the beds lay a little child asleep, and his arm hung down from the bed, and I saw the ring upon his hand. On the side of the bed sat a woman; I thought I had seen her before, so I looked again all the closer, and I knew that it was the same that I had seen in the tent, offering up her two children with joy to be the servants of the king. Then I looked for her ring; it was safe upon her hand, and sparkling brighter than ever. By her stood a little boy, just cleanly washed and dressed, though his clothes were rough and poor.

THE TENT ON THE PLAIN

I looked into the little one's face, and I saw it was the same child which had been led by the hand in the tent; but it seemed as if two or three years had passed by since then, for he was grown now into a boy. His mother was speaking to him. She told him that he was the king's servant, nay, his child. She told him that when he was little, she and his father had given him to serve the king, and she said how good it was of the king to take such children to be his. Then she bade him ask the king's help that he might faithfully serve him that very day.

So the little fellow looked up with a mild face, bent his bare knees, and raised his hands which he had folded together, while he spoke as his mother taught him. And as he put up his hands, I could see his ring. There it was, safe upon his finger, and it was just beginning to sparkle, so that any one could mark it.

Then methought my guide touched me again, and we stood in another cottage. It was something larger than the last, and the things that were in it were not so coarse as those I had just seen. But although they were finer, they did not please me as well, for they were dirty and all unmended.

There stood in the room we were in a woman whose face I had seen before. I cast about, until

THE TENT ON THE PLAIN

I bethought me that she was one of the careless ones on whom the king's minister had looked very sadly, and to whom he had spoken words of warning when she came with her husband and her children to be entered in the king's book. By her side stood a boy who had then been with her; bigger he was than the little one in the cottage we had just left; but there was no sparkling light on his ring; and alas! when I looked at it nearer, I could see that it was moved far from where it had been put upon his finger. His mother had just taken him up, and was dressing him; and I heard her say that he was "an idle boy," and in a rough voice she bid him "be quick"; and then she hurried him downstairs, and never asked help of the king herself nor bid him ask for it either; and when she raised her hand to open the latch of the door, I saw that her ring was quite dull, and nearer off her finger than that of the poor boy.

My heart was very sad at such a sight, and whilst I was musing on it, my guide asked me, " Wouldst thou see yet more?" When I said "Yes," he led me forth, and lo! it was mid-day, and we stood upon the village green, and the boys of the village were playing around us; but they saw us not, because the invisible mantle was on me. Then I saw, amongst the rest, the two boys I had seen in the morning, but I marked no difference between them, for they sported and played about like the rest.

Then the man took from under his cloak a wonderful glass, and he bade me look through it at the boys as they played. Now the glass made hidden things plain; for as soon as I looked through it, I saw around the boys that the air was full of ugly and venomous creatures, who were the king's enemies. As I looked at them through the glass, it seemed as if their names were written upon them, and I could read on one, "bad thoughts," and on another, "peevishness," and on another, "anger," and on another, "bad words," and on another, "deceit," and on another, "greediness," and on the most hateful-looking of all, which had a long venomous tongue and a slimy nature, I could read the word "lie." Then I saw that these were very busy amongst the boys as they played, that they came near to them, and "anger" would push one boy against another, to make them quarrel; and "bad thoughts" would fly there directly, and bring "bad words" with them, and they would all hover about them, and help on the quarrel, without the boys seeing or knowing they were there. I saw "greediness," too, lead some of the boys near to fruit-trees, on which hung rich and

ripe fruit, which they had been told not to touch,
and then "deceit" would whisper to them that
nobody would know it, though they should take
a little. Then I watched to see how the boys
behaved, and I saw the little one whose ring was
dull in the morning, take of the forbidden fruit,
and eat, and then listen to the words of the
wicked "deceit"; and then the hateful "lie"
came close to him, and I saw it curl all round
the little boy's heart, and his ring got deader
and deader, and seemed ready to fall from his
finger. Then I saw him offer some of the fruit
to the other little one I had seen in the morning.
But he shook his head, and drove "greediness"
away, and would not hear a word that "deceit"
wanted to whisper; for he said, "I must not tell
a lie, and take what is forbidden me, for I am
the king's child, and the king sees all I do."
I saw that as he named "the king," the hateful
creatures fled away, and his ring seemed firmer
than ever on his finger, and began to shine and
sparkle the brighter. So then I knew how even
little children could serve the king, and fight
against his enemies.

Then again my guide touched me, and he
said, "Follow me"; so I followed him forth, and
we soon stood in the midst of a great city,
and we passed along its crowded streets. Houses

were on this side, and houses on that; and the clear air was made thick with the smoke of chimneys, and the dust of the streets, but still my guide led me on and on. At last we came to a narrower and more dirty street. Tall old houses, which looked ready to fall, almost touched one another over the narrow road. Dirty children, who looked pale and wretched, screamed in many of the rooms, or sat in a sad sort of sorrowful play, on the dirty steps of the houses; and dirty men and women talked loud, and I heard many bad words as I walked along. By one of the dirtiest and worst of all the houses my guide stopped, and we stood within it. No one saw us, for the mantle was on me; and oh, what a sad sight did I see! There were many in the room, for a whole family lived in it, and they were wicked people; bad words came out of their mouths as often as they spoke, and they quarrelled and almost fought, and looked as though they hated one another. And now I saw that there was in one corner of this room, near to a broken window, a sad-looking bed, in which lay a poor sick boy, who seemed about ten years old. He was very pale and very thin, and there was a bright red spot upon his cheek, and he coughed very often, and seemed in pain. His face was turned towards the window, and his eyes were

bent down upon the bed. As I leaned over to
see what he looked at, I saw he was reading in
a book, and heard him whisper to himself the
words, "Forsake me not when my strength faileth
me." Then I saw that it was in the king's book
that he was reading, and I heard that he was
speaking to the king, and asking HIM to keep
him; and I saw that his ring was so bright and
sparkling, it seemed like a little ball of living
fire. Then my guide bade me look through the
glass; and what a sight did I see! All round
his bed I could see beautiful forms of heavenly
creatures, which the king had sent to watch
over him. "Promises" were there with kind
eyes and soft voices whispering ever in his ears.
"Patience" held his aching head in her lap, and
"Hope" was holding a bright crown just over
his head, and telling him how soon he would be
able to wear it.

Oh, how sad was it to turn round from the
happy bed of the dying child, to the rest of that
sinful room!—to look on the dark faces of evil
men and women, and to hear their evil words,
instead of looking at the mild glad faces of the
angel-friends of the little one, and catching the
soft words with which they cheered his soul!
But my guide bade me mark these people well;
and I saw that all their rings were dull—dull as

if they were dead, and well-nigh off their fingers.
More than one seemed to have lost their rings
altogether, and one I heard boasting that he
never had been happy till he had thrown his
away; but when I looked at him through the
glass, I saw " Misery,'' and " Sorrow," and
" Hatred" sucking his heart's blood, and the
dreadful face of " Despair" coming nigher and
nigher to him every moment.

And now I thought within myself, how can
the child of such parents have learned to serve
the king faithfully? My guide answered my
thoughts, and he told me that "once his ring
too had seemed dead and well-nigh taken from
his finger; but it pleased the king to send a holy
man to warn him, and he gave to him the book
you have seen him read : and there came with
it a sweet air from the king's presence which
' bloweth where it listeth,' and the boy began to
read in the book and love it. And as he read
he learned to call to the king earnestly for help;
and then his ring began to settle on his finger,
and the shining of the stone to come out—and
now look at him again, and see his happiness
in sorrow."

Then I looked again through the glass, and
more was showed me than before. But a little
above his bed methought there was a golden

door, not wholly closed. And I could see within it a light more beautiful than sunshine, which came from a throne whose lowest golden steps I could see, and on the top of which, as I doubted not, sat the great king himself. Hundreds and thousands of beautiful and happy creatures were there. Some I took for angels, and some methought had once been men and women. But all wore shining crowns, and all were blessed and happy.

Then as I gazed, methought the door opened wider, and I saw the gentlest of all those heavenly beings fly down to the sick boy's bed; and "Mercy" was written on her brow. She stretched out her hand, and he arose, and flew up with them to the golden door; and I could hear a burst of happy music as they entered, and I saw a bright crown reached out. And the face of the dead boy (for I looked into his bed, and he breathed no more) shone with the bright light of that heavenly temple!

Then I awoke from my vision; but my thoughts still stayed with me, and I saw how good it was to be the soldier of the king, and to fight his battles faithfully.

THE ROCKY ISLAND

AND

OTHER PARABLES

"Feed my lambs."—ST JOHN xxi. 15.

NOTE TO THE PRESENT EDITION.

"The Rocky Island, and other Parables" was begun in January, 1840, and published towards the close of that year. This second book was not received with such unanimous favour as the first, and the author became the object of accusations which he deeply resented (*Life*, vol. i. pp. 158, 215 foll.). It has never had quite the same popularity as "Agathos," but it has even more of the author's ease and grace of style, and of his skill in representing character. Perhaps if he had not published the questions and answers which followed the stories, and which are omitted in this reprint, the little book would have met with fewer objections.

A. J. M.

PREFACE.

THE advertisement to a work of a similar character to the present expresses the author's principle and wishes as to this little volume. It is constructed on the same plan, and, like the former, has had the test of the observations of his own children on its parables before it was given to the public. The reception of "Agathos" has shown that many parents have felt the want which these little volumes are intended to supply, and leads the author to hope that he has in some measure been able to meet it.

It is a peculiar gratification to him to be able thus to enter many a Christian household, and fulfil, in some measure, his Master's charge, "Feed my lambs."

May it please God to give His blessing to this new attempt.

S. W

WINCHESTER.

THE ROCKY ISLAND

I SAW in my dream a rough rocky island
rising straight out of the midst of a roaring sea.
In the midst of the island rose a black steep
mountain; dark clouds rested gloomily upon its
top; and into the midst of the clouds it cast
forth ever and anon red flames, which lit them
up like the thick curling smoke at the top of a
furnace-chimney. Peals of loud thunder sounded
constantly from these thick clouds; and now and
then angry lightning shot its forked tongue, white,
and red, and blue, from the midst of them, and
fell upon the rocks, or the few trees which just
clung to their sides, splitting them violently
down, and scattering the broken and shivered
pieces on all sides. It was a sad, dreary-looking
island at the first view, and I thought that no
one could dwell in it; but as I looked closer at
its shores, I saw that they were covered with
children at play. A soft white sand formed its
beach, and there these children played. I saw
no grown people among them; but the children
were all busy—some picking up shells; some
playing with the bright-coloured berries of a

117

prickly dwarf-plant which grew upon those sands;
some watching the waves as they ran up and
then fell back again on that shore; some running after the sea-birds, which ran with quick
light feet along the wet sand, and ever flew off,
skimming just along the wave-top, and uttering
a quick sharp note as the children came close
upon them. So some sported in one way, and
some in another, but all were busily at play.
Now I wondered in my dream to see these
children thus busy whilst the burning mountain
lay close behind them, and the thunder made
the air ring.

Sometimes, indeed, when it shone out redder
and fiercer than usual, or when the thunder
seemed close over their heads, the children
would be startled for a little while, and run together, and cry, and scream; but very soon it
was all forgotten, and they were as full of their
sports as ever.

While I was musing upon this, I saw a man
appear suddenly amongst the children. He was
of a noble and kingly countenance, and yet so
gentle withal that there was not a child of them
all who seemed afraid to look in his face, or to
listen to his kind voice when he opened his
mouth, for soon I found that he was speaking
to them. "My dear children," I heard him say,

THE ROCKY ISLAND

"you will all be certainly killed, if you stay upon this rocky island. Here no one ever grows up happily. Here all play turns into death; the burning mountain and the forked lightning, and the dreadful breath of the hill-storm—these sweep down over all that stay here, and slay them all; and if you stay here, for these childish pleasures of yours, you will all perish."

Then the children grew very grave, and they gazed one upon another, and all looked up into the face of the man to see if he spoke in earnest. They saw directly that he did, for that kind face looked full of care as well as of love : so from him they looked out upon the waves of the sea, and one whispered to another, " Where shall we go? how shall we ever get over that sea? we can never swim across it ; had we not better go back, and play and be happy, until the time comes for us to die?"

" No," said the man, looking round kindly upon them all ; "you cannot swim over; you never could get over of yourselves: but you need not stay here and die ; for I have found a way of escape for you. Follow me, and you shall see it."

So I saw that he led them round a high rough rock, to where the calm waves of the sea ran up into a little bay, upon the white sand of which only a gentle ripple broke with a very pleasant sound. This bay was full of boats, small painted boats, with just room in each for one person, with a small rudder to guide them at the stern, and a little sail as white as snow, and over all a flag, on which a bright red cross was flapping in the gentle sea-breeze.

Then, when the children saw these beautiful boats, they clapped their little hands together for very joy of heart. But the man spoke to them again and said : "You will all have a deep, and dangerous, and stormy sea to pass over in these little boats. They will carry you quite safely, if you are careful to do just as I bid you, for then neither the wind nor the sea can harm them ; but they will bear you safely over the foaming waves to a bright and beautiful land— to a country where there is no burning mountain, and no angry lightning, and no bare rocks, and no blasting hill-storm ; but where there are trees bearing golden fruits by the side of beautiful rivers, into which they sweep their green boughs. There the trees are always green, and the leaves ever fresh. There the fruit ripens every month, and the very leaves upon the trees are healing. There is always glad and joyful light. There are happy children who have passed this sea ; and there are others who have grown old full of

happiness ; there are some of your fathers, and
mothers, and brothers, and sisters ; and there am
I ever present to keep and to comfort you."

Then all the children were for jumping into
the boats, and he was kindly ready to help them,
only he put each one in carefully and slowly ;
and as he put him in, he gave him his charge.
He told them that they must never look round
to this island they were leaving, but must be
always setting their faces towards the happy
land they sought for. He told them that they
must leave behind them all the shells and the
berries which had pleased them here, for if they
tried to take these with them in their boats,
some accident would certainly befall them. Then
some of the children, when they heard all this,
drew secretly away, and ran round the point,
and gave up the boats and the sea, and began
their old idle play again. And some of them,
I thought, hid the shells and the berries they
had got, and then jumped into the boat, pre-
tending they had left all behind them.

Then I saw that the man gave different
presents to each of them, as they seated themselves in the boat. One was a little compass
in a wooden box. "This," he said, "will always
show you which way to steer ; you are to follow
me, for I shall always be before you on the

waters ; but often when the darkness of night comes on, or the thick mist seethes up from the wave's brim, or the calm has fallen upon you so that your boat has stood still—often at such times as these you may not be able even to mark my track before you : then you must look at the compass, and its finger will always point true and straight to where I am ; and if you will follow me there you will be safe." He gave them, too, a musical instrument which made a soft murmuring sound when they breathed earnestly into it. "And this," he said, "you must use when there is a calm round you so that you cannot get on, or when the waves swell into a storm around you and threaten to swallow you up." He gave them, too, bread and water for many days.

So I saw that they all set out upon their voyage, and a beautiful sight it was to look upon. Their snow-white sails upon the deep sea shone like stars upon the blue of the firmament ; and now they all followed close upon the leader's ship, and their little boats danced lightly and joyfully over the trackless waves which lifted up their breasts to waft them over : and so they started. But I looked again in a little while, and they were beginning to be scattered very widely asunder : here and there three or

THE ROCKY ISLAND

four of the boats kept well together, and followed steadily in the track of the leader's vessel;
then there was a long space of the sea with no
boat upon it at all; then came a straggler or
two, and then another company; and then, far
off on the right and on the left, were other boats,
which seemed to be wandering quite away from
the leader's path.

Now, as I watched them closer, I saw that
there were many different things which drew
them away. One I saw, soon after they started,
who turned back to look at the rocky island,
forgetting the man's command. He saw the
other children playing on the beach; he heard
their merry voices; and then looking round
again towards the sea, it looked rough and dark
before him; and he forgot the burning mountain,
and the terrible thunder, and the bright happy
land for which he was bound, and the goodly
company he was in, and the kind face of the
kingly man; and he was like one in a dream,
before whose eyes all sorts of shapes and colours
fly, and in whose ears all sounds are ringing;
and he thought no more of the helm, nor watched
the sails; and so the driving swell carried his
boat idly along with its long roll; and in a few
minutes more I saw it at the top of a white
foaming breaker, and then he and it were dashed

123

down upon the rocks which girdled the sandy beach, and he was seen again no more.

Then I turned my eyes to two other boats, which were going fast away from the true course, for no reason which I could see; but when I looked at them more closely, I saw that they were in a sort of angry race; each wished to get to the wind-side of the other; and they were so busy thinking about this, and looking at one another with angry glances, and calling out to one another with angry words, that they forgot to look for the leader's ship, or to watch the finger of the compass; and so they were going altogether wide of the track along which they should have passed.

Then I looked closely at another, which was shooting quite away in another direction; and I saw that the poor child had left the rudder, and was playing with something in the bottom of the boat; and as I looked nearer in it, I saw that it was with some of the bright berries of the rocky island which he had brought with him that he was so foolishly busy.

Foolish, indeed, he was; and kind had been the warning of the man who bade them leave all these behind; for whilst I was watching him, and wondering what would be the end of such a careless voyage, I saw his little boat strike

suddenly upon a hidden rock, which broke a
hole in its wooden sides, and the water rushed
in, and the boat began to sink, and there was
no help near, and the poor boy was soon drowned
in the midst of the waves.

Then I turned sadly away to watch the boats
which were following their leader; and here,
too, I saw strange things; for though the sea
when looked at from afar seemed just alike to
all, yet when I watched any one, I saw that he
had some difficulties, and some frights, and some
helps of his own, which I did not see the others
have.

Sometimes it would fall all at once quite dark,
like a thick night, all round a boat; and if he
that was in it could hear the voice of a companion near him for a little while, that gladdened
him greatly; and then oftentimes all sound of
voices died away, and all was dark, still, deep
night, and he knew not where to steer. Now if,
when this fell upon him, the child went straight
to his compass, and looked close upon it in spite
of the darkness, there came always a faint
flashing light out of the darkness, which played
just over the compass, so as to shew him its
straight blue finger, if he saw no more; and
then, if he took up his musical instrument, and
blew into it, though the thickness of the heavy

air seemed at first to drown its sound, yet, after awhile, if he was but earnest, I could hear its sweet murmuring sound begin; and then directly the child lost his fears, and did not want company; sweet echoes of his music talked with his spirit out of the darkness, and within a little time the gloom would lift itself quite up again, or melt away into the softest light: and lo! he had got far on his voyage even in this time of darkness, so that sometimes he could see the beloved form just before him; and at times even the wooded shore of the happy land would lift itself up, and shine on his glad eyes, over the level brim of the silver sea.

From another boat it would seem that the very air of the heaven died away. There it lay, like a painted sail in a picture—the snow-white canvas drooping lazily, or flapping to and fro, as the long dull swell heaved up the boat, and let it sink again into the trough of the waves: other boats, but a little way off, would sail by with a full breeze; but he could not move; his very flag showed no sign of life. Now if the little sailor took to amusing himself when this happened, it seemed to me that there he lay, and would lie, till the dark night overtook him, and parted him from all his company. But if, instead of this, he took up his musical instrument, and played upon it with all his earnestness, its soft breath, as it whispered to the wind, soon woke up its gentle sighing; the long flag lifted itself up; the blood-red cross waved over the water; the snowy sails swelled out, and the little boat danced on along its joyful way.

I noticed also that before those boats which were passing on the fastest, the sea would every now and then look very dark and threatening. Great waves would seem to lift their white heads just before them; whilst everywhere else the sea looked calm and enticing. Then the little sailor would strain his eye after his master's course, or look down at the faithful compass; and by both of these sure signs he saw that his way lay straight through these threatening waves. Well was it for him if, with a bold heart and a faithful hand, he steered right into them. For always did I see, that just as he got where it seemed to be most dangerous, the tossing waves sank, as if to yield him an easy passage; the wind favoured him more than at any part of his voyage; and he got on in the right way faster than ever before. Especially was this so, if at first he was somewhat tossed, and yet held straight on; for then he shot into a glassy calm, where tide and wind bore him steadily along into the desired haven. But sad was it for him if,

instead of then trusting to the compass, he
steered for the smoother water. One or two
such trembling sailors I especially observed.
One of them had long been sailing with the
foremost boats; he had met with less darkness,
fewer mists or troubled places, than the boats
around him; and when he saw the white crests
of the threatening waves lift up their strength
before him, his heart began to sink; and after
wavering for a moment, he turned his little boat
aside to seek the calmer water. Through it he
seemed to be gliding on most happily, when all
at once his little boat struck upon a hidden
sand-bank, and was fixed so firmly on its side,
that it could not get afloat again. I saw not
his end; but I sadly feared that when next the
sea wrought with a troubled motion, and the
surf broke upon that bank, his little boat must
soon be shivered, and he perish in the waves.

The other who turned aside followed closely
after him; for this was one thing which I noted
through all the voyage. Whenever one boat
went astray, some thoughtless follower or other
would forget his compass to sail after the unhappy wanderer; and it often happened that
these followers of others went the farthest wrong
of any. So it was in this case; for when the
first boat struck upon the sand-bank, the other,

thinking to escape it, bore still farther off ; and so chancing to pass just where the shoal ended, and an unruly current swept by its farthest edge, the boat was upset in a moment, and the poor child in it drowned.

And now I turned to three or four boats which had kept together from the time they left the harbour. Few were forwarder than they; few had smoother water or more prosperous gales. I could see, when I looked close into their faces, that they were all children of one family ; and that all the voyage through they were helping, cheering, and directing one another. As I watched their ways, I noticed this, too, which seemed wonderful. If one of them had got into some trouble with its tackle, and the others stayed awhile to help it, and to bring it on its way, instead of losing ground by this their kindness, they seemed all to make the greater progress, and press on the farther in their course.

And now I longed to see the ending of this voyage ; and so, looking on to those which were most forward, I resolved to trace them to the end.

Then I found that all, without exception, came into a belt of storms and darkness before they reached the happy land. True, it was much rougher and more dark with some than others; but to every one there was a deep night and a troubled sea. I saw, too, that when they reached this place, they were always parted one from another. Even those which had kept most close together all the voyage before, until just upon the edge of this dark part, they, like the rest, were scattered here, and toiled on awhile singly and alone.

They seemed to me to fare the best who entered on it with the fullest sails, and had kept hitherto the straightest course. Indeed, as a common rule, I found this always true— that those who had watched the compass, and held the rudder, and cheered themselves with the appointed music, and eaten the master's bread, and steered straight after him, they passed through this cloud and darkness easily and swiftly.

Next to these were those who sought most earnestly to cheer its horrors with the sound of their appointed music. The Lord of these seas, indeed, had many ways of cheering his followers. Even in the thickest of that darkness his face of beaming love would look out upon them; and he seemed nearer to them then than he had done heretofore through all their voyage.

Then, moreover, it was never long, and bright light lay beyond it. For they passed straight out of it into the haven where they would be. Sweet sounds broke upon their glad ears even as they left that darkness. A great crowd of happy children—parents who had gone before them—friends whom they had loved, and holy persons whose names they had long known— these all lined the banks, waiting to receive and welcome them. Amidst these moved up and down shining forms of beautiful beings, such as the children's eyes had seen only in some happy dream ; and they, too, were their friends ; they, too, waited for them on the bank ; they, too, welcomed them with singing, and bore the happy new-comer with songs of triumph into the shining presence of the merciful King. Then, on the throne royal, and with the glorious crown upon his head, they saw the same kind face of gentle majesty which had looked upon them when they played on the shores of that far rocky isle. They heard again the voice which had bid them fly the burning mountain. They saw him who had taken them into his convoy ; who had given them their boats ; who had been near them in the storm ; who had given them light in the darkness ; who had helped them in the dull calm ; who had never left them ; but who had kept and guided them across the ocean, and who now received them to his never-ending rest.

THE VISION OF THE THREE
STATES

I SAW, in my vision, two glorious creatures
walking together through a beautiful garden.
I thought at first they must be angels, so bright
and happy did they seem. The garden, also, in
which they were, seemed too beautiful for earth.
Every flower which I had ever seen, and numbers
which my eye had never looked upon, grew in
abundance round them. They walked, as it were,
upon a carpet of flowers. The breeze was quite
full of the rich scent which arose from them. The
sun shone upon them with a brightness such as
I had never seen before; whilst the air sparkled
with the beautiful butterflies and winged things
which flew here and there, as if to show how
happy they were.

All through the garden, too, I saw every sort
of beast, in all its natural grace and beauty; and
all at peace. Great lions moved about amongst
tender sheep; and striped tigers lay down quietly
to sleep amongst the dappled fawns which sported
around them. But, amidst all these beautiful

sights, my eyes followed, more than all, the two
glorious forms which were walking together with
such a kingly majesty through the happy garden:
they were, truly, I could see, beings of this earth;
they were talking to each other; they were speaking of ONE who had made them out of the dust
of the earth; who had given to them living souls;
who was their Father and their Friend; who had
planted for them this beautiful garden, and made
them the rulers of all that was in it.

Now I marked them as they talked, and I
could see that their eyes were often turned from
all the beauty round them towards one far end
of the garden; and as I watched them, I saw
that they were still passing on towards it. Then
I also fixed my eyes there, and in a while I could
see that, at the end of the garden to which they
were moving, there was a bright light, brighter
and purer than the light of the sun; and I thought
that in it I could see here and there heavenly
forms moving up and down, flying upon silver
wings, or borne along upon the light breath of
the sunny air. But as I strained my eyes to
pierce into it, it seemed to dazzle and confound
them by its great lustre. Then again I heard
the words of the two; and they spake of what
was before them; of the bright light, and the
heavenly forms; and I found that they were only

133

travellers through this beautiful garden; that the
King who had placed them in it dwelt in that
light, the brightness of which had so confounded
my gaze; that they were on their way to his
presence, and that when they reached it, they
should be happy for ever; even as those shining
spirits were already, whose golden figures I had
been just able to discover.

Now, whilst I was pondering upon these
things, and casting my eyes round and round
this beautiful garden, I heard all at once a most
terrible sound, as of thunder, such as man's ears
had never heard. I looked up, and the bright
light at the end of the garden seemed to turn
itself into an angry fire, and to flash red and
threatening through thick black clouds, which
were forming themselves into terrible shapes all
over the garden. Then I looked for the two that
I had seen before: I could just see them; sorrow
sat upon their faces, and fear made them deadly
pale; a serpent was gliding from them into the
bushes; and their eyes were fixed upon the air,
as though voices, which I heard not, were speaking terrible things to their inner ears. Then, as
I looked, it grew darker and darker—the thunder
pealed all round me—cries came forth from every
hill, as of fierce and deadly beasts in wild dreadful
fight. The flowers round me were withering up,

as if a burning blight had passed over them; and soon it was all dark, and dreary, and desolate.

Then, when my heart was very heavy within me, methought there stood by me one of the forms of light whom I had seen at the garden's end; and my knees smote together through fear of his glory; but he looked upon me kindly, and spoke to me in a voice of pity, and he said, "Wouldst thou see the end of this sight?" Then my heart gathered courage, and I told him that if it were lawful, I would indeed fain look upon it.

With that he lifted me, and we flew through the air, and I knew not where he had borne me; but in a while he set me on my feet, and bade me look right down beneath me. Then I looked down at his word, but could see nothing. My eyes seemed to rest upon the thick mantle of the night, and they could not pierce through it. Now, while I was striving to look into that darkness, strange noises rose from it to my ears. All sounds that ever were, came up from it, so mingled together that I could not say what they were—whether it were a groan, or a cry, or a roaring, or music, or shouting, or the voice of anger or of sorrow; for all of these seemed joined together into one; but the groaning was louder than the laughing, and the voice of crying well-nigh drowned the music. Then I asked my guide what was this strange noise; and he told me that it was the voice of all the world, as it rose up to the ears of those that were on high. Then I begged of him, if it might be, to let me see those from whom it came. With that he touched my eyes; and now methought, though the darkness remained, that I could see in the midst of its thickness, even as in the brightness of the day.

It was a strange place into which I looked. Instead of the beautiful garden I had seen before, and two glorious creatures passing through it, now I saw a multitude of men, women, and children, passing on through a waste and desolate wilderness. Here and there, indeed, there were still flowery spots, but they were soon trodden down by the feet of those who passed along. Strange, too, were their steps. Now, instead of passing straight on, they moved round and round, for they were all in the black darkness. The ground was full of pitfalls, in the low bottoms of which I could see red fire burning fierce and hot, and one after another fell over into these pitfalls, and I saw them no more. Evil beasts, too, moved amongst them, slaying one, and tearing another; and as if this was not enough, oftentimes they would quarrel and fight with one another, until the ground all around was covered with their bodies strewed upon it.

136

Yet for all this, some would sing and dance, and frolic; and this seemed to me to be the saddest of all, for they were like madmen; and mad in truth they were, for in the midst of their dancing and their singing one and another would get near the side of some great pitfall, and step over into its flames, even with the song upon their lips.

In vain did I strain my eyes to see any light at the end, as I had seen it in the garden. If it was there, the black clouds had rolled over it so thick and dark that not a ray of it was left.

Yet I heard one and another offering to lead those that would follow them safely through this terrible wilderness; and such men never wanted followers: so I watched many of these leaders, to see what they would do for those that trusted them. Little help could any of them render. Some put their followers on a path which led straight down into the deepest and most frightful pitfalls; some set them on a path which wandered round and round, and brought them at the end back to the same place from which they started; some led them into thorny places, where the poor pilgrims pierced their bleeding feet with many a wound: but not one did I see who brought them into any better place, or took them any nearer to their journey's end.

THE VISION OF THE THREE STATES

How they found their way at all was at first
my wonder. But as I looked more closely, I saw
in all their hands little lanterns, which just threw
a feeble light upon the darkness round them.
These were always brightest in the young, for
they soon grew very dim ; and the falls and blows
they met with bruised and shattered them so
much, that some had hardly any glimmering left,
even of the feeble light which they had seemed
to cast of old.

I looked at them until my heart was very
sad, for there was no peace, no safety, no hope ;
but all went heavily and sadly, groaning and
weeping, or laughing like madmen, until, sooner
or later, they seemed all to perish in the fearful
pitfalls !

Then my angel-guide spoke to me again,
marking my sadness, and he said, " Hast thou
well observed this sight ? " and I answered, "Yes."
Then he said, "And wouldst thou see more ? "
So when I had said "Yes," methought we were
flying again through the air, until again he set
me on my feet, and bid me look down. Now
here, too, strange noises reached my ears ; but
as I listened to them, methought there were mixed
with them such sounds as I had not heard before.
Sweet clear voices came up now from the din,
speaking, as it were from one close by me, words

of faith, and of hope, and of love; and they sounded to me like the happy talking which I had heard at the first between the glorious beings in the garden.

So when my guide touched my eyes, I bent them eagerly down into the darkness below me.

At first I thought that it was the same place I had seen last, for there was a busy multitude passing to and fro; and there were music and dancing, and sobbing and crying; there were pitfalls, too, and wild beasts. But as I looked closer, I saw that, in spite of all this, it was not the place that I had seen before. Even at a glance I could see that there were many more flowers here than there; and that many amongst the pilgrims were going straight on, with happy faces, by a road which passed safely by all the pitfalls. I could see, too, that at the end of the road was a dim shining of that happy light which had been so bright in the beautiful garden.

Now, as I looked, I saw that there were but a few who kept to this straight safe road, and that many were scattered all over the plain. I saw many leave this path even as I looked upon it; and very few did I see come back to it: those who did, seemed to me to find it very hard to get into it again; whether it was that its sides were slippery, or its banks so steep, many fainted and gave up, after trying to climb into it again. But it seemed quite easy to leave it; for every one who left it went on at first lightly and pleasantly. Sometimes, indeed, they seemed greatly startled after taking their first step out of it, and some of them turned straight back, and after a few struggles, more or less, such always got into it again. But if once after this first check they set out for the plain, they seemed to go easily along, until their path lay straight by the den of some destroying beast, or led them into the midst of the pitfalls, where they wholly lost their reckoning, and knew not how to get on, or how to get back.

I saw, too, after a while, that they had got lanterns in their hands, some of which gave a great deal of light. Those which were carried along the narrow path shot out bright rays on all sides, until towards the end they quite blazed with light. I could see, too, that these travellers had some way of trimming and dressing their lamps; and that much of their light seemed to come from an open book which they carried in their hands, from the leaves of which there flashed out continually streams of light, which made their lamps burn so brightly that all their road shone with it. But as they got further and further from the path, their lamps began to burn dim. All these travellers, too, had the book of light closed; or if they now and then opened it, they shut it up again, some carelessly, and some as if its light frightened them; and not one could I see who stopped to trim his light: so that just when they got amongst the pitfalls, and wanted light the most, they were all the most nearly in darkness.

Now, when I had looked at them for a space, and wondered, my guide said to me, "Wouldst thou see how they enter on this plain?" Then he took me to a fair porch, which came from the wilderness I had looked upon before; and there I saw a man standing in white robes, and speaking good words, and giving good gifts to each one as he came in. There were persons coming in of all nations and people, and some, too, of all ages, though the greatest number were little children, so small that their little hands would not hold the man's gifts, and so he hung them round their necks, for them to use as soon as they were able.

Then I joined myself to the group, to hear and see the better what was passing. The man in white was speaking with a grave kind voice as I came up. He told the pilgrims that the great Lord of the land had built that porch, and set him there to help the poor travellers, who were before without hope or help amongst the beasts, and snares, and pitfalls of the terrible wilderness; he told them that the blood of the King's own son had been shed, that that porch might be built; that the King had prepared them a narrow way to walk in, which led straight from that porch to his own blessed presence, and that they might all pass along it safely if they would; he told them that if they left that path, they would surely get again amongst the pitfalls which they had left in the wilderness; nay, that they would be worse off than they had been even there, for that there was no other porch where they could again be set right, and no other place where the gifts that he was giving them now could ever be got any more, if they were once thrown quite away.

Then I looked to see what these gifts were. I saw the man bring forth clear and sparkling water, which shone as if with living light; and with this he washed from them the dirt and the bruises of the terrible wilderness: with this, too, he touched their little lamps, and as it touched them, they grew so bright and clear, that the light within poured freely forth on all around them. Then he looked in their faces, and gave them a name, which he wrote down in the King's book; and he told them, that by this name they should be known, not only by their fellow-

travellers, but that this would remain written
in the King's book here, unless they wholly left
his path; and that every name which remained
written here, they would find written in another
book in letters of gold and of fire, when they
reached the other end of the path; and that for
every pilgrim, whose name was written there, the
golden gate would open of itself, and he would
find a place and a crown in the presence of the
King.

Then, as he spoke all these glorious words,
my heart burned within me to see how the
travellers sped.

But he had not yet done with them; for he
brought out of his stores a golden vial for each
one; and he told them that in it the King had
stored the oil of light and beauty for the dressing
of their lamps.

Then he showed them how to use it; not
carelessly or lightly, for then the oil would not
flow; but earnestly, and with great care; and
then sweet odours issued from the vial; and the
flame of the lamp burned brightly and high. He
gave them, too, the precious light-book, which
I had seen; and he bade them read in it when it
was dark, or the way was slippery; and that they
should ever find that it was a lantern unto their
feet, and a light unto their paths. He put, too,

into the hand of each a trusty staff, suited to their age ; and then he told them, while they leant upon it, it would bear them up at many a pinch, and ever grow with their growth, and strengthen with their strength. "Church-truth" he called these staffs ; and they were made after a marvellous fashion, for they were as if many wands had been woven together to make one ; and as I looked, I could see "example," and "experience," and "discipline," and "creeds," written upon some of these wands, which grew together into "Church-truth."

Then I longed greatly to follow forth some of these whom I had seen under the porch; and as I gazed, I saw the man look earnestly into the face of a fair boy who stood before him : he gave him the name of "Gottlieb[1]," and entered it in the book, and put the staff in his hand, and washed him with living water, and hung the vial at his side, and put the banded staff into his hands ; and, bidding him God-speed, set him out upon his journey.

Then he looked steadily into the face of another, and it, too, was fair to look upon ; but it had not the quiet happy peace of the last. The man wrote it down as "Irrgeist[2]"; and I thought

[1] Love of God.   [2] Wanderer.

a shade of sadness swept over his brow as he gave to him the King's goodly gifts.

Then he sent forth a third, whose timid eye seemed hardly firm enough for so long a journey; and I heard the name that was given him, and it was "Furchtsam[1]." Close to him went another, with a firm step, and an eye of steady gentleness; and I saw, by the King's book, that he bore the name of "Gehülfe[2]."

So these four set out upon their journey; and I followed them to see how they should fare. Now, I saw that at first, when they started, they were so small that they could not read in the goodly book, neither could they use the golden vials; and their little banded sticks would have fallen from their hands if they had not been small and thin, like the first green shoots of the spring. Their lamps, too, cast no light outwardly, yet still they made some way upon the path; and whilst I wondered how this might be, I saw that kind hands were stretched out of the darkness round them, which held them up and guided them on their way.

But, anon, in a while they were grown larger; and I could see Gottlieb walking on the first, and his book of light was open in his hand, and his

---

[1] Timid. [2] Help.

lamp burned bright, for he often refreshed it with
oil, and he leant upon his good staff, and strode
along the road.

Then, as he walked on, I saw that there stood
upon his path a shadowy figure, as of one in
flowing robes, and on her head she seemed to
wear a chaplet of many flowers; in her hands
was a cup of what seemed to be crystal water,
and a basket of what looked like cool and refreshing fruit. A beautiful light played all round her,
and half shewed her and her gifts to the boy.
She bid him welcome, as he came up to her; so
he raised his eyes from his book, and looked to
see who spoke to him. Then she spoke kindly
to him; and she held forth the cup towards him,
and asked him if he would not drink. Now, the
boy was hot with walking, for the air was close,
so he stretched out his hand to take the cup; but
though it seemed so near to him, he could not
reach it. And at the same moment she spake to
him again, and asked him to come where these
fruits grew, and where the breeze whispered
amongst the boughs of yonder trees—and there
to drink and rest, and then go on his way again.
Then I saw that she had power to call out of the
darkness the likeness of all she spoke of. So he
looked at the trees to which she pointed; and the
sun seemed to shine around them, and the shade

146

looked cool and tempting under them, and the pleasant breeze rustled amongst their fresh leaves; and he thought the road upon which he was travelling was hotter and darker, and more tiring than ever; and he put up his hand to his burning brow, and she said to him, as he lingered, "Come." Now, the trees to which she pointed him lay off his road, or he would gladly have rested under them; and whilst he doubted what to do, he looked down to the book that was open in his hand; and the light shot out upon it bright and clear, and the words which he read were these, "None that go unto her return again, neither take they hold of the paths of life." And as he read it, he looked again at the stranger; and now he could see more clearly through the wild light which played around her, and he knew that it was the evil enemy who stood before him; the sparkling cup, too, and the fruit, turned into bitter ashes; and the pleasant shady grass became a thorny and a troublesome brake: so, pushing by her with the help of his staff, he began to mend his pace; and looking down into the book of light, there shone out, as in letters of fire, "Wherewithal shall a young man cleanse his way? by taking heed thereto according to thy word."

Then I saw that he was feeding his lamp,

which had begun to grow dim as he parleyed with the tempter, and that he ceased not till it streamed out as bright and as clear as ever.

But still the air was hot and sultry, and no cool breath blew upon him; and if he looked off for a moment from his book, the fair form of the tempter stood again beside him in silver light; the cold water sparkled close to his lips; and trees with shady boughs waving backward and forward over fresh green grass, and full, in every spray, of singing birds, seemed to spring up around him. For a little moment his step faltered: but as his lamp streamed out its light, all the vain shadows passed away; and I heard him say, as he struck his staff upon the ground, "I have made a covenant with my eyes"; and even as she heard it the tempter passed away and left him to himself. Scarcely was she gone, before he passed by the door of a beautiful arbour. It was strewn with the softest moss; roses and honeysuckle hung down over its porch; a bright light, as from a living diamond, streamed softly down from its roof; and in the midst of its floor, a clear, cool, sparkling stream of the purest water bubbled ever up from the deep fountain below it. Now, as this lay on the road, Gottlieb halted for a moment to look at it; and the light of his lamp waxed not dim, though he thus stayed to see it; the book of fire, too, spoke to him of rest, and of halting by "palm trees and wells of water"; and as he looked, he read in letters of light over the doorway:

> "Faithful pilgrim, banish fear,
> Thou may'st enter safely here;
> Rest for thee thy Lord did win;
> Faithful pilgrim, enter in."

Then Gottlieb rejoiced greatly, and cast himself gladly upon the mossy floor, and bent down his parched lips to drink of the cool spring which bubbled up before him.

Now, whilst he was resting safely here, I turned to see how it fared with the others who had set out with him from the porch, for they had not got as far as Gottlieb.

The first of them was Irrgeist; and when I looked upon him he was drawing near to the place where Gottlieb had fallen in with the tempter. Irrgeist was walking quickly on—so quickly that, at the first glance, I thought he would soon be by the side of Gottlieb. But, upon looking more closely, I saw that Gottlieb's steps had been far more steady and even than those with which Irrgeist was pressing on; for Irrgeist's lamp burned but dimly, and gave him

no sure light to walk in. Very near to the place
where Gottlieb had met with her, the tempter
stood beside Irrgeist. He was not looking at
his book, as the other had been; and he did not
wait to be spoken to; for as soon as he saw the
light which played round her figure, he began
to speak to her, and asked who she was. She
told him that her name was "Pleasure"; and
forthwith she shewed to him her crystal cup and
fruits; and she brought before the charmed eyes
of the wanderer all the gay show with which she
had tried before to mislead the faithful Gottlieb.
There was the bright sunshine, and the green
path, and the waving trees, and the rustling of
the wind, and the song of birds, and the sweet
resting-shade. Irrgeist looked eagerly at all she
shewed him, and in his haste to reach out his
hand for the cup, he dropped altogether the
trusty staff of "Church-truth." Then the cup
seemed to draw away from him, just as it had
done from Gottlieb; but he followed thought-
lessly after it. And soon I saw that he left the
path upon which he had been set; and though
he started suddenly as soon as he was off it, yet
it was but a moment's start,—the cup was close
before him, the shadowy form led him on, the
grass was green, and the trees and the sunlight
but a little farther.

And now I saw him drink some of the en-
chanted water; and as he drank it, his look grew
wild, and his cheek burnt like the cheek of one
in a fever; and he walked after the deceitful
figure with a quicker step than ever: but I saw
that his lamp was almost out, that the book of
living light had fallen from his hands, and the
golden vial hung down, ready, as it seemed, to
fall from him altogether.

Still he walked on; and a strange flitting
light, from the form which was before him,
lightened the darkness of the valley, so that he
could pass on quickly; the meadow, also, was
smooth and even, and there was a rustling
breeze, which played around him: so that he
got on faster than he had ever done upon the
narrow path, and thought that he was getting
well on to his journey's end.   Many times did
he put forth his hand for the sparkling cup, and
drank of it again and again.

But now I saw, as I thought, a strange change
which was coming over him; for he drank oftener
of the bowl, but appeared each time to find it
less refreshing.   Sometimes it seemed almost
bitter, and yet he could not but take it the very
moment he had thrust it from him.   The shadowy
form, also, before him, seemed altogether altering;
he looked again, and her beautiful features and

151

pleasant countenance had changed into a sharp, stern, and reproachful frown. His own voice, which had been heretofore almost like one singing, grew sad and angry. The very figure of his guide seemed vanishing from his eyes: the light which floated round her grew wilder and more uncertain, and his own lamp was almost out. He felt puzzled and bewildered, and hardly knew which way to go: he had got into a broad beaten path, and he found that many besides himself were going here and there along it. Sometimes they sang; and, in very grief of heart, he tried to sing too, that he might not think: but every now and then, when a flashing light came, and he saw the look of the travellers amongst whom he was, it made his very heart shiver—they looked so sad and so wretched. Now, none went straight on: some turned into this path, some into that; and then he soon lost sight of them altogether. Sometimes he heard fearful cries, as if wild beasts had seized them; sometimes a dreadful burst of flame from the fearful pits which I had seen, made him fear that they had fallen over into them: for poor Irrgeist had got now into the midst of the deep pits and the ravenous beasts. And soon he found how terrible was his danger. He had been following one who had made him believe that he had light to guide his steps; he had gone with him out of the beaten path; and they were pressing on together, when Irrgeist suddenly lost sight of him in the darkness; and whether it was that he had fallen into a pit, or become the prey of some evil beast, poor Irrgeist knew not; only, he found that he was more alone than ever, and near to some great peril. Poor Irrgeist sprang aside with all his force, thinking only of the danger which he feared; but, feeling his feet slipping under him, he turned, and saw that he had got upon the treacherous brink of a fearful pit; down which, at the very moment, another pilgrim fell. The fierce red flames rose out of it with a roar like thunder, and a blaze like the mouth of a furnace; and the wind blew the flames into the face of Irrgeist, so that he was singed and almost blinded by this blaze. Then the poor boy called in the bitterness of his heart upon Pleasure, who had led him out of the way, and now had forsaken him; but she came no more—only terrible thoughts troubled him; and he heard the hissing of serpents as they slid along in the bushes near him, and all evil noises sounded in his ears, till he scarcely knew where he was standing. Then he thought of his staff, which he had dropped when Pleasure had first tempted him, and he grieved that it was

153

gone; and he felt in the folds of his mantle, hoping that he might still have the book of light within it; for he had too often thrust it there at the beginning of his journey; but he could not find it. Then he strove to get some light from his little lamp; for, hurt as it was, he had it still in his hand, and he thought there was just a little blue light playing most faintly within it; but this was not enough to direct him on his way, rather did it make his way more dark. Then, at last, he bethought him of the golden vial. Few were there of those near him but had lost theirs altogether, and his hung only by a single thread. But it was not gone; and when he had striven long, he just drew from it a single drop of oil, and he turned his lamp, and it yielded forth a little trembling light, just enough to shew that it was not altogether dead. With the help of this light, he saw that when he had dropped his book of fire, one single leaf had been torn from it, and stuck to his mantle; so he seized it eagerly, and strove to draw light from it; but all that it would yield was red and angry looking light, and all that he could read was, "The way of transgressors is hard."

Poor Irrgeist! he sat down almost in despair, and wept as if his heart would break. "Oh, that I had never trusted Pleasure!" "Oh, that

I had never left the path!" "Oh, that I had
my book of light, and my lamp's former brightness, and my goodly stick!" "Oh, that one
would lighten my darkness!"

Then did it seem to me as if in the murmur
of the air around him two voices were speaking
to the boy. One was like the gentle voice of the
man whom I had seen at the porch of the valley;
and it seemed to whisper "return," "return";
"mercy," and "forgiveness." And then something like hope mixed with the bitter tears which
ran down the face of the wanderer. But then
would sound the other voice, harsh, and loud,
and threatening; and it said, "too late," "too
late," "despair," "despair," "despair."

So the poor boy was sadly torn and scattered
in his thoughts by these two different voices;
but, methought, as he guarded his golden vial,
and strove to trim his dying lamp, that the
gentle voice became more constant, and the
voice of terror more dull and distant.

Then, as I was watching him, all at once the
boy sprang up, and he seemed to see a light
before him, so straight on did he walk; many
crossed his path and jostled against him, but
he cared not; he heard the sweet voice plainer
and plainer, like the soft murmuring of the
cushat dove in the early summer, and he would

follow where it led. Hitherto his pathway had
been smooth, and he had hastened along it;
but this did not last, for now it narrowed almost
to a line, and ran straight between two horrible
pitfalls; so he paused for a moment; but the
roaring of a lion was behind him, and forward
he pressed. It was a sore passage for Irrgeist,
for the whole ground was strewed with thorns,
which pierced his feet at every step, and the
sparks from the fire-pits flew ever around him,
and now and then fell in showers over him.
Neither did he hear now the pleasant sound of
the voice of kindness; whether it were that it
had died away, he knew not, or whether it were
that the crackling and roaring of the fierce
flames, and the voice of the beasts behind, and
his own groans and crying, drowned its soft
music, so that he heard it not.

I had looked at him until I could bear it no
more; for the path seemed to grow narrower and
narrower; the flames from the two pits already
almost touched; and I could not endure to see,
as I feared I should, the little one whom I had
watched become the prey of their devouring
fierceness. So, with a bitter groan for Irrgeist,
I turned me back to the road to see how it
fared with Furchtsam and Gehülfe.

They had fallen far behind the others from

the first. Poor little Furchtsam had a trembling, tottering gait; and as he walked, he looked on this side and on that, as if every step was dangerous. This led him often to look off his book of light, and then it would shut up its leaves, and then his little lamp grew dimmer and dimmer, and his feet stumbled, and he trembled so, that he almost dropped his staff out of his hands. Yet still he kept the right path, only he got along it very slowly and with pain.

Whether it was that Gehülfe was too tender-spirited to leave him, or why else, I know not, but he kept close by the little trembler, and seemed ever waiting to help him. Many a time did he catch him by the hand when he was ready to fall, and speak to him a word of comfort, when without it he would have sunk down through fear. So they got on together, and now they came to the part of the pathway which the evil enchantress haunted. She used all her skill upon them, and brought up before their eyes all the visions she could raise; sunshine, and singing-birds, and waving boughs, and green grass, and sparkling water, they all passed before their eyes—but they heeded them not; once, indeed, poor Furchtsam for a moment looked with a longing eye at the painted sun-

shine, as if its warm light would have driven off
some of his fears; but it was but for a moment.
And as for Gehülfe, whether it was that he was
reading his book of light too closely, or trimming
too carefully his lamp, or helping too constantly
his trembling friend, for some cause or other he
scarcely seemed to see the visions which the
sorceress had spread around him. So when she
had tried all her skill for a season, and found it
in vain, she vanished altogether from them, and
they saw her no more. But their dangers were
not over yet. When Gottlieb passed along this
road, he had gone on so boldly, that I had not
noticed how fearful it was in parts to any giddy
head or fainting heart. But now I saw well how
it terrified Furchtsam. For here it seemed to
rise straight up to a dangerous height, and to
become so narrow at the same time, and to be
so bare of any side-wall or parapet, that it was
indeed a giddy thing to pass along it. Yet when
one walked over it, as Gottlieb did, leaning on
his staff of Church-truth, reading diligently in
his book, and trimming ever and anon his lamp,
such a light fell upon the narrow path, and the
darkness so veiled the danger, that the pilgrim
did not know that there was anything to fear.
But not so when you stopped to look—then it
became terrible indeed ; you soon lost all sight

158

of the path before you; for the brightest lamp only lighted the road just by your feet, and that seemed rising almost to an edge, whilst the flash of distant lights here and there shewed that a fearful precipice was on each side.

Furchtsam trembled exceedingly when he looked at it; and even Gehülfe, when, instead of marching on, he stopped to talk about it, began to be troubled with fears. Now, as they looked here and there, Furchtsam saw an easy safe-looking path, which promised to lead them in the same direction, but along the bottom of the cliffs. Right glad was he to see it; and so, taking the lead for once, he let fall his staff, that by catching hold of the bushes on the bank, he might drop down more easily upon the lower path; and there he got with very little trouble.

It was all done in a moment; and when he was out of the path, Gehülfe turned round and saw where he was gone. Then he tried to follow after him; but he could not draw his staff with him through the gap, or climb down the bank without letting it go. And happily for him, he held it so firmly, that after one or two trials he stopped. Then, indeed, was he glad, as soon as he had time to think; and he held his good stick firmer in his hand than ever, for now he saw plainly that Furchtsam was quite out of the road, and that he had himself well-nigh followed him. So leaning over the side, he began to call to his poor timid companion, and encourage him to mount up again by the bank which he had slipped down, and venture along the right way with him. At first Furchtsam shook his head mournfully, and would not hear of it. But when Gehülfe reminded him that they had a true promise from the King, that nothing should harm them whilst they kept to the high way of holiness, and that the way upon which he had now entered was full of pitfalls and wild beasts, and every sort of danger, and that in it he must be alone—then his reason began to come back to him, and Furchtsam saw into what an evil state he had brought himself; and with all his heart he wished himself back again by the side of Gehülfe. But it was no such easy matter to get back. His lamp was so bruised and shaken as he slid down, that it threw scarcely any light at all; and he thought it had never seemed so dark as it did now; he could not see the bushes to which he had clung but now, or the half path which had brought him down. Gehülfe's voice from above was some guide to him, and shewed him in which direction to turn; but when he tried to mount the bank, it was so steep and so slippery, he could scarcely cling to it; and he had no staff to lean upon, and no friendly hand to help him. Surely, if it had not been for the kind, encouraging voice of Gehülfe, the weak and trembling heart of Furchtsam would have failed utterly, and he would have given up altogether.

Now, just at this time, whilst he was reaching out to Furchtsam, and urging him to strive more earnestly, he heard a noise as of one running upon the path behind him; and he looked round and saw one of the King's own messengers coming fast upon it; so when he came up to Gehülfe, he stopped and asked him what made him tarry thus upon the King's path. Then Gehülfe answered very humbly, that he was striving to help back poor Furchtsam into the right way, from which he had been driven by his fears. Then the messenger of the King looked upon him kindly, and bid him "fear not." "Rightly," he said, "art thou named Gehülfe, for thou hast been ready to help the weak; and the Lord, who has bidden his children to bear one another's burdens, has watched thee all along thy way, and looked upon thee with an eye of love; and forasmuch as thou seemest to have been hindered in thy own course by helping thy brother, the King has sent me to carry thee on up this steep place, and over this dangerous road." With

M   161   11

that, I saw that he lifted up the boy, and was about to fly with him through the air. Then, seeing that he cast a longing look towards the steep bank, down which Furchtsam had slipped, and that the sound of his sad voice was still ringing in his ear, the King's messenger said to him, "'Cast thy burden upon the Lord.' 'The Lord careth for thee.' 'For the very hairs of your head are numbered,' and 'the Lord is full of compassion, pitiful, and of great mercy.'" So the heart of Gehülfe was soothed, and with a happy mind he gave himself to the messenger, and he bore him speedily along the dangerous path, as if his feet never touched the ground, but refreshing airs breathed upon his forehead as he swept along, and silver voices chanted holy words to his glad heart. "He shall gather the lambs in his arms," said one; and another and a sweeter took up the strain and sang, "and he shall carry them in his bosom." And so he passed along the way swiftly and most happily.

Then I saw that he bore him to the mouth of the arbour, into which Gottlieb had turned to rest. And now as he came up to it, Gottlieb was just coming forth again to renew his journey. Right glad was Gottlieb of the company of such a comrade, so they joined their hands together, and walked along the road speaking to one an-

162

other of the kindness of the King, and telling one
to the other all that had befallen them hitherto.
It was a goodly sight to see them marching along
that road, their good staffs in their hands, their
lamps burning brightly, and their books sending
forth streams of light to shew them the way that
they should go.

But now I saw they got into a part of the road
which was rough and full of stones; and unless
they kept the lights they bore with them ever
turned towards the road, and looked, too, most
carefully to their footing, they were in constant
danger of falling. The air, also, seemed to have
some power here of sending them to sleep, for
I saw that Gottlieb's steps were not as steady
and active as they had been; and he looked often
from this side to that, to see if there were any
other resting-place provided for him; but none
could he see: and then methought, as he walked
on, his eyes would close as he bent them down
over his book, like one falling asleep from exceeding weariness.

Gehülfe saw the danger of his friend; and
though he felt the air heavy, his fear for Gottlieb
kept him wide awake. "What are those words,"
he asked his drowsy friend, "which burn so
brightly in your book?" When he heard the
voice, Gottlieb roused himself, and read; and it

163   11—2

was written, "Watch and pray, lest ye enter into temptation; the spirit truly is willing, but the flesh is weak." Then, for a little while, Gottlieb was warned, and he walked like one awake; but, after a time, such power had this sleepy air, he was again almost as drowsy as ever, and his eyes were almost closed. Then before Gehülfe could give him a second warning, he placed his foot in a hole, which he would have easily passed by if he had been watching; and, falling suddenly down, he would have rolled quite out of the road (for it was raised here with a steep bank on either side) if Gehülfe had not been nigh to catch him again by the hand, and keep him in the path. He was sorely bruised and shaken by the fall, and his lamp, too, was dusted and hurt; so that he could not, at first, press on the way as he wished to do. But now his drowsiness was gone; and, with many bitter tears, he lamented that he had given way to it before. One strange thing I noted, too: he had dropped his staff in his fall, and he could not rise till he had taken it again in his hand; but now, when he tried to take it, it pricked and hurt his hand, as if it had been rough and sharp with thorns. Then I looked at it, and saw that one of the stems which were twined together, and which bore the name of "discipline," was very rough and thorny; and this, which had

turned inwardly before, was now, by his fall,
forced to the outside of the staff, so that he must
hold that or none. Now I heard the boy groan
as he laid hold of it; but lay hold of it he did,
and that boldly, for he could not rise or travel
without it, and to rise and travel he was determined. Then he looked into his book of light,
and he read out of it these words, "Make the
bones which thou hast broken to rejoice." And
as he read them he gathered courage, and made a
great effort, and stood upon his feet, and pressed
on beside Gehülfe.

Then I saw that the road changed again, and
became smoother than they had ever known it.
Gottlieb's staff, too, was now smooth and easy in
his hand, as it had been at first. Soon also a
pleasant air sprung up, and blew softly and yet
cool upon their foreheads. And now they heard
the song of birds, as if the sunshine was very
near them, though they saw it not yet. There
were, too, every now and then, sounds sweeter
than the songs of birds, as if blessed angels
were near them, and they were let to hear their
heavenly voices. A little further, and the day
began to dawn upon them—bright light shone
on some way before them, and its glad reflection
was already cast upon their path. But still there
was one more trial before them; for when they

had enjoyed this light for a season, and I thought they must be close upon the sunshine, I saw that they had got into greater darkness than ever. Here, also, they lost sight of one another; for it was a part of the King's appointment, that each one must pass that dark part alone—it was called the shadow of death. Gehülfe, I saw, walked through it easily; his feet were nimble and active, his lamp was bright, his golden vial ever in his hand, his staff firm to lean upon, and the book of light close before his eyes: he was still reading it aloud, and I heard him speak of his King as giving "songs in the night"—and so, with a glad heart, he passed through the darkness. The brightest sunshine lay close upon the other side of it; and there he was waited for by messengers in robes of light, and they clad him in the same, and carried him with songs and music into the presence of the King.

But Gottlieb did not pass through so easily. It seemed as if that darkness had power to bring out any weakness with which past accidents had at the time affected the pilgrim; for so it was, that when Gottlieb was in it, he felt all the stunning of his fall come back again upon him, and, for a moment, he seemed well-nigh lost. But his heart was sound, and there was One who was faithful holding him up: so he grasped his good staff tighter than ever, though its roughness had come out again and sorely pricked his hand; but this seemed only to quicken his steps; and when he had gone on a little while thus firmly, as he looked into his book he saw written on its open page, "I will make darkness light before thee." And as he read them, the words seemed to be fulfilled, for he stepped joyfully out of the darkness into the clear sunlight. And for him too messengers were waiting; for him, too, were garments ready woven of the light; around him were songs, and music, and rejoicing; and so they bare him into the presence of the King.

Now, when I had seen these two pass so happily through their journey into rest, I thought again of the poor trembling Furchtsam, and longed to know that he had got again into the road. But upon looking back to where I had lost sight of him, I saw that he was still lying at the foot of the steep bank, down whose side he had stepped so easily. He had toiled and laboured, and striven to climb up, but it had been all in vain. Still he would not cease his labour; and now he was but waiting to recover his breath to begin to strive again. He was, too, continually calling on the King for aid. Then I saw a figure approaching him in the midst of his cries. And poor Furchtsam trembled exceedingly, for he was

of a very timorous heart, and he scarcely dared
to look up to him who stood by him. Then the
man that stood by him asked him in a grave, pitying voice, "What doest thou here?" Then the poor
boy sobbed out in broken words the confession
of his folly, and told how he had feared and left
the road, and how he had laboured to get back
into it, and how he almost thought that he should
never reach it. Then I saw the man look down
upon him with a face of tenderness and love;
and he stretched forth his hand towards him;
and Furchtsam saw that it was the hand that
had been pierced for him; so he raised the boy
up, and set him on his feet; and he led him
straight up the steepest bank. And now it seemed
easy to his steps; and he put him back again in
the road, and gave the staff into his hand, and
bid him "redeem the time, because the days are
evil": and then he added, "Strengthen ye the
weak hands, and confirm the feeble knees. Say
to them that are of a fearful heart, Be strong;
fear not." Such strength had his touch, his
words, and his kind look given to the heart of
the timid boy, that he seized the staff, though its
most prickly "discipline" sorely hurt his tender
flesh; and leaning on it, he set bravely out without a moment's delay. And I heard him reading
in his book of light as he climbed up the steep

168

path which had affrighted him; and what he read was this: "Before I was afflicted I went wrong; but now have I kept thy word."

When he had almost reached the arbour, another danger awaited him; for he saw, as he thought, the form of an evil beast lying in the pathway before him. Then did some of his old terrors begin to trouble him; and he had turned aside, perhaps, out of the way, but that the wholesome roughness of his staff still pricked his hand and forced him to recall his former fall. So instead of turning aside, he looked into his book of light, and there he read in fiery letters, "Thou shalt go upon the lion and the adder; the young lion and the dragon shalt thou tread under thy feet"; and this gave him comfort. So on he went, determining still to read in his book, and not to look at all at that which affrighted him; and so it was, that when he came to the place, he saw that it was only a bush, which his fears had turned into the figure of a beast of prey; and at the same moment he found where it was written in his book, "No lion shall be there, nor any ravenous beast shall go up thereon, it shall not be found there; but the redeemed shall walk there."

And now he stood beside the arbour, where he rested awhile, and then pursued his journey. Now I noticed, that as he got further on the road, and read more in his book, and leant upon his staff, he grew bolder and firmer in his gait; and I thought that I could see why Gehülfe, who had been needful to him in his first weakness, had afterwards been carried away from him; for surely he had leant more upon him, and less upon his book and his good staff, unless he had walked there alone.

However this might be, he grew continually bolder. As he drew near the last sad darkness, I began again to tremble for him; but I need not have done so; for he walked on so straight through it, that it seemed scarcely to make any difference to him at all. In the best part of the road his feebleness had taught him to lean altogether upon him who had so mercifully helped him on the bank, and who had held up his fainting steps hitherto; and this strength could hold him up as well even in this extreme darkness. I heard him, as he passed along, say, "When I am weak, then am I strong"; and with that he broke out into singing:

> "Through death's dark valley without fear
>   My feeble steps have trod:
> Because I know my God is near;
>   I feel his staff and rod."

With that he too passed out of the shade and

darkness into the joyful sunshine. And oh, it was indeed a happy time! It made my heart bound when I saw his face, which had so often turned pale and drooped with terror, now lighted up with the glow of the heavenly light; when, instead of the evil things which his fears had summoned up, I saw around him the bands of holy ones, and the children of the day: and so they passed along. And soon, I thought, he would see again the hand which had been stretched out to save him on the bank, and hear the kind and merciful voice which had soothed his terror and despair, and live in the present sunshine of that gracious countenance.

And now methought I heard an earnest and sorrowful voice, as of one crying aloud for help; so I turned me round to see where he was that uttered it, and by the side of the King's path I could see one striving to mount the bank, and slipping back again as often as he tried. He was trying in right earnest; his cries were piteous to hear, and he laboured as if he would carry his point by storm. But it was all in vain; the more he struggled, the worse his case grew; for the bank, and all the path up to it, got so quagged and miry with his eager striving, that he seemed farther and farther from getting safely up. At last, as he was once more struggling violently

171

up, his feet quite slipped from under him, and
he fell upon his side; and so he lay sobbing and
struggling for breath, but still crying out to the
King, who had helped him before, and delivered
him from the flames of the pit, to help him once
more, and lift him again into the right way. My
heart pitied the poor boy, and I looked more
closely into his face, and saw that it was Irrgeist
—not Irrgeist as he had been when he had walked
at first with Gottlieb along the road, or as he had
been when he had first followed the deceitful
phantom " Pleasure " out of it—but Irrgeist still,
though brought by his wanderings and his trouble
to paleness, and weariness, and sorrow. Now,
whilst I was looking at him, as he lay in this
misery, and longing for some helper to come to
him, lo, his cries stopped for a moment, and
I saw that it was because One stood by him
and spoke to him. Then I could see under the
mantle, which almost hid him, that it was the
same form which had visited Furchtsam, and
delivered him when he had cried. Now, too,
I saw the hand held out, and I saw Irrgeist seize
it; and it raised him up, and he stood upon his
feet: and the staff was given to him—exceeding
rough, but needful and trusty; and his lamp
shone out, and the book of light was his: and
his feet were again in the road.

But I marked well that Irrgeist trod it not as the others had done. Truly did he go along it weeping. Whether it was that the thought of what he had gone through amongst the pitfalls dwelt ever on his mind; or whether it were shame of having wandered, I know not,—but his road seemed evermore one of toil and sorrow. Still, in the midst of tears, a song was often put into his mouth, and his tongue was ever speaking of the great kindness of him who had restored the wanderer; his head, too, was so bowed down, that he marked every stone upon the road, and therefore never stumbled; but still his speed was little, and his troubles were many. When he got to the dark part, he had a sore trial; his feet seemed too weak and trembling to bear him; and more than once I heard him cry out, as if he thought that he were again between the pitfalls, and the fire were ready to break out upon him. But then did it seem as if there were some sweet hopes given him, and his face brightened up; and in a faint, feeble voice, he would break out again into his song and thanksgiving. As he drew towards the end, things somewhat mended with him; and when he was just upon the sunlight, and began to see its brightness through the haze, and to hear the voices of the heavenly ones, methought his heart would have burst, so did it beat with joy; and withal he smote upon his breast, and said: "And this for me! And this for the wanderer! Oh mercy, choicest mercy! Who is a God like unto thee, that pardonest iniquity?" And so saying, he entered on the heavenly light, and left for ever behind him the darkness and the danger of the pitfalls, and the face of shame, and the besetting weakness; for he, too, was clothed in raiment of light, and borne with joy before the Lord the King.

THE LITTLE WANDERERS

In a miserable little hovel, built on the edge
of a wide and desolate common, lived a poor
widow woman, who had two sons. The eldest
of them was quite young, and the least was
scarcely more than an infant. They were dressed
in torn and dirty rags, for the widow had no
better clothes to put upon them; and often they
were very hungry and very cold, for she had
not food or fire with which to feed and warm
them. No one taught the biggest boy anything;
and as for the poor mother, she did not know
a letter. She had no friends; and the only play-
fellows the little ones ever knew were other
children as poor, and as dirty, and as untaught,
as they were themselves, from whom they learnt
nothing but to say bad words and do naughty
tricks. Poor children! it was a sad life, you
would say, which lay before them.

Just at this time the widow was taken very ill
with a fever. Long she lay in that desolate hut,
groaning and suffering, and no one knew how ill
she was but the little children. They would sit

and cry by her miserable bed all day, for they were very hungry and very sad. When she had lain in this state for more than a week, she grew light-headed, and after a while died. The youngest child thought she was asleep, and that he could not waken her; but the elder boy was frightened, and ran screaming out of the house.

Just at that very moment a man passed by, who looked into the pale, thin, hungry face of the sobbing child, with a kind, gentle look, and let himself be led into the wretched hut, where the poor dead mother lay. His heart bled for the poor orphans, for he was one who was full of tenderness; so he spake kind words to them; and when his servants came up after a while, he gave orders that their dead mother should be buried, and that the children should be taken from the miserable hut, to dwell in his own beautiful castle.

To it the children were moved. The servants of the Lord of the castle put on them clean fresh clothes—washed their old dirt from them; and as no one knew what were their names, they gave them two new names, which showed they belonged to this family; and they were cared for, and given all they wanted.

Happy was now their lot. They had all they

176

wanted; good food in plenty, instead of hunger and thirst; clean raiment, instead of rags and nakedness; and kind teachers, who instructed them day by day as they were able to bear it. There were a multitude of other happy children too in the castle, with whom they lived, and learned, and spent their glad days. Sometimes they played in the castle, and sometimes they ran about in the grounds that were round it, where were all sorts of flowers, and beautiful trees full of singing birds, and green grass, and painted butterflies; and they were as happy as children could be.

All over these grounds they might play about as they would; only on one side of them they were forbidden to go. There the garden ended in a wide waste plain, and there seemed to be nothing to tempt children to leave the happy garden to walk in it, especially as the kind Lord of the castle bid them never set foot on it; and yet it was said that some children had wandered into it, and that of these, many had never come back again. For in that desert dwelt the enemies of the Lord of the castle; and there was nothing they loved better than to pounce down upon any children whom he had taken as his own, and carry them off, to be their slaves in the midst of the waste and dreary sands.

THE LITTLE WANDERERS

Many ways, too, had these enemies of enticing the children to come on the plain; for as long as they stayed within the boundary, and played only in the happy garden, the enemy could not touch them. Sometimes they would drop gay and shining flowers all about the beginning of the waste, hoping that the children would come across the border to pick them up; and so it was, that if once a child went over, as soon as he had got the flower for which he had gone into his hands, it seemed to fade and wither away; but just beyond him he thought he saw another, brighter and more beautiful; and so, too, often it happened that, throwing down the first, he went on to take the second; and then, throwing down the second, he went on to reach the third; until, suddenly, the enemy dashed upon him, and whirled him away with them in a moment.

Often and often had little Kühn[1]—for so the eldest boy had been named—looked out over this desert, and longed, as he saw the gay flowers dropped here and there, to run over the border and pick them up. His little brother, who was now old enough to run about with him, would stand and tremble by him as he got close to the desert; but little Zart[2] would never leave him; and sometimes, I am afraid, they would

[1] Bold, or rash.   [2] Tender.

have both been lost, if it had not been for a
dear little girl, who was almost always with
them, and who never would go even near to the
line. When Kühn was looking into it, as if he
longed for the painted flowers, the gentle Glaube[1]
would grow quite sad, and bending her dark
sorrowful eyes upon him, their long lashes would
become wet with tears, and she would whisper
in a voice almost too solemn for a child, "Oh,
Kühn, remember!" Then Kühn, who could not
bear to see her sad, would tear himself away;
and the flowers seemed directly to lose their
brightness, and the desert looked dry and hot,
and the garden cool and delicious, and they
played happily together, and forgot their sorrow.

But it was very dangerous for Kühn to go so
near. The servants of the Lord of the castle
often told the children this; and seeing a bold
and daring spirit in Kühn, he had been told it
over and over again. What made it so dangerous
was this—that the flowers of the wilderness never
looked gay until you got near its border, but it
seemed dusty, dry, and hot; but the nearer you
got to it, the brighter shone the flowers; they
seemed also to grow in number, until you could
hardly see its dry, hot sands for the flowery
carpet that was drawn over them.

[1] Faith.

THE LITTLE WANDERERS

Poor Kühn! he was often in danger. Never
yet had he crossed the border; but it is a sad
thing to go near temptation; and so this unhappy
child found to his cost.

One day he was sauntering close to the forbidden border, when the hoop which he was
trundling slipped from him and ran into the
desert. In a moment he was over after it; and
just as he stooped to pick it up, he saw, right
before him, a beautiful and sparkling flower.
He would certainly have gone after it, but that
at the instant he caught the eye of Glaube
looking sadly after him, and it struck upon his
heart, and he hastened back, and was safe. For
a while his legs trembled under him, and Zart
looked up quite frightened into his pale face;
Glaube, too, could scarcely speak to him; and
it was long before they were laughing merrily
again under the tall palm-trees of the garden.
But by the next day all Kühn's fears had flown
away, and he went with a bolder foot than ever
to the very edge of the desert.

Glaube was further off than usual; and just
as Kühn and Zart were in this great danger, a
beautiful bird started up under their feet. The
boys had never seen such a bird. All the colours
of the rainbow shone upon his feathers, and his
black and scarlet head seemed quite to sparkle

in the sunshine. It tried to fly; but whether its wing was hurt, or what, I know not, but it could not rise, and ran before them flapping its painted wings, screaming with a harsh voice, and keeping only just before them. The boys were soon in full chase, and everything else was forgotten : when, just as they thought the bird was their own, he fluttered across the border, and both the boys followed him—Kühn boldly and without thought, for he had been across it before ; but poor little Zart trembled and turned pale, and clung to his bolder brother, as if he never would have crossed it alone.

Once over, however, on they went, and the bird still seemed to keep close before them ; and they never noticed how far they were getting from the garden, when all at once they heard a dreadful noise: the air looked thick before them, as if whole clouds of dust were sweeping on ; shining spear-heads were all they could see in the midst of the dust; and they heard the trampling of a multitude of horses. The boys were too much frightened to shriek, but they clung to one another, pale and trembling, and ready to sink into the earth. In a minute rude hands seized them ; they heard rough voices round them ; and they could see that they were in the midst of the enemies of the Lord of the castle. In another minute they were torn asunder, they were snatched up on horseback, and were galloped off towards the sad home in which the evil men of the desert dwelt. In vain the boys cried, and begged to be taken home; away galloped the horses, and not a word of all their begging and cries was listened to. They had gone on long in this way, and the dark-frowning towers of the desert castle were in sight. The little boys looked sadly at one another; for here there was no flowering garden, there were no sheltering trees, but all looked bare, and dry, and wretched; and they could see little narrow windows covered with iron bars, which seemed to be dungeon-rooms, where they thought they should be barred in, and never more play together amongst the flowers and in the sunlight.

Just at this moment the little Zart felt that, by some means or other, the strap which bound him to the horse had grown loose, and in another moment he had slipped down its side, and upon his head on the ground. No one noticed his fall; and there he lay upon the sand for a while, stunned and insensible. When he woke up, the trampling of horses had died away in the distance; the light sand of the desert, which their feet had stirred, had settled down again like the heavy night-dew, so that he could see no trace of their footmarks. The frowning castle-walls were out of sight; look which way he would, he could see nothing but the hot flat sand below, and the hot bright sun in the clear sky above him. He called for his brother, but no voice answered him; he started up, and began to run he knew not where; but the sun beat on his head, the hot sand scorched his weary feet; his parched tongue began to cleave to his mouth: and he sank down upon the desert again to die.

As he lay there he thought upon the castle-garden and its kind Lord; upon the sorrowful face with which Glaube was used to look on them, when he and Kühn drew near to the forbidden border; and his tears broke out afresh when he thought of his brother in the enemies' dungeon, and himself dying in the desolate wilderness. Then he called upon the Lord of the castle, for he remembered to have heard how he had pitied wandering children, and heard their cry from afar, and had brought them back again to his own happy castle. As he lay upon the sand, crying out to the Lord of the castle, he thought that he heard a footstep, as of one walking towards him. Then there came a shade between the sun and his burning head, and looking languidly up, he saw the kind face of

the Lord of the castle turned towards him. He
was looking on the poor child as he had looked
on him when he had pitied him by the side of
the hut; and that kind face seemed to speak
comfort. Then he stretched out to him his hand,
and he bade him rise; and he lifted up the child,
and bore him in his bosom over that waste and
scorching wilderness, nor ever set him down until
he had brought him again into the pleasant
garden. Once, as he lay in that bosom, Zart
thought that he heard in the distance the tramp-
ing of horse-hoofs; and he saw the dusty cloud
lifting itself up; but he felt that he was safe;
and so he was, for the enemy did not dare to
approach that Mighty One who was bearing him.

When he reached the garden again, the gentle
Glaube met him, and welcomed him back again
to their peaceful home. But he hung down his
head with shame and with sorrow; and as he
looked up into the face of the Lord of the
garden, he saw in it such kindness and love, that
his tears rolled down his cheeks to think how he
had broken his command, and wandered into the
wilderness of his enemies. Then he tried to
speak for his brother, for his heart was sore
and heavy with thinking of him; but the Lord
of the castle answered not. Many, many days
did Glaube and Zart pray for him; but they

heard nothing of him; whether he died in the
enemies' dungeon; or whether, as they still dared
to hope, he might even yet one day find his way
back to the garden of peace; or whether, as
they sometimes trembled to think, he had grown
up amongst the enemies of their Lord, and
become one of them—they knew not, and they
dared not to ask. But they never thought of
him without trembling and tears, and Zart more
even than Glaube; for he had crossed that
terrible border; he had been seized by the fierce
enemy; he had lain alone in the wide scorching
desert; and had only been brought back again
from death by the great love of the mighty and
merciful Lord of that most happy garden.

THE KING AND HIS SERVANTS

[St Matthew xxv 14—30]

A GREAT king once called his servants to
him, and said to them—"You have all often
professed to love me, and to wish to serve me;
and I have never yet made trial of you. But
now I am about to try you all, that it may be
known who does in truth desire to serve me,
and who is a servant only in name. To-morrow
your trial will begin; so meet me here in the
morning, and be ready to set out upon a journey
on which I shall send you."

When the king had so spoken, he left them;
and there was a great deal of bustle and talking
amongst these servants. Not that they were all
alike. Some were very busy, and said a great
deal of the services they should render; and that
they hoped it would be some really hard trial on
which the king would set them. Others were
quiet and thoughtful, saying little or nothing,
but, as it seemed, thinking silently of the words
the king had spoken, as if they feared lest they

should fail in their trial. For they loved that
king greatly ; he had been as a father to them
all. Once they had been slaves, and cruelly
treated by a wicked tyrant who had taken them
prisoners, and cast some of them into dungeons,
and made others work in dark mines, and dealt
evil with them all. But the king had triumphed
over this their enemy, and rescued them from
his hands. His own son had sought them in
the dungeons and dark pits into which they had
been cast, and had brought them out; and now
he had given them places in his service, and
fed them from his own kingly table; and he
promised to such as were faithful, that he would
raise them yet higher; that he would even set
them upon thrones, and put crowns upon their
heads; and that they should remain always in
his presence, and rule and dwell with him. Now,
when the time of their trial was come, these
faithful servants were grave and thoughtful,
fearing lest they should fail, and be led to forget
him, their kind and gracious king. But one
thought held them up. He had said unto them
all, "As your day, so shall your strength be."
They knew, therefore, that he would put on them
no task beyond their strength. They remembered his kindness and his love in taking them
out of the dungeons of the enemy. They desired

greatly to serve him; and so they rejoiced that
their trial was come, even while they feared it;
and they trusted in him to help them, even whilst
they trembled for themselves.

These servants spent much of the night in
preparing for their journey, in thinking over all
the directions the King had ever given them;
for many times had he spoken to them of this
coming trial, and even written down plain
rules for them, which should teach them always
how he would have them act. All these they
gathered together, lest in the hurry of setting
out they should forget any one of them; and so
they went into the court of the palace to meet
the king.

Then he came forth from his palace-door and
gave them all their charge.

From the great treasure-chambers of that
palace he brought out many different gifts, and
laid them before these his servants. One had
gold and silver, and another had precious stuffs;
but all had something good and costly; and as
he gave them these gifts, he told them that this
was to be their trial. He was about to send
them with these gifts into an exceeding great
and rich city, which lay afar off from his palace;
and in that city they were all to trade for him.
They were to take his gifts and use them wisely,

so that each one of them might bring something back to him. He gave them also very close and particular instructions. He told them there were many in that city who would try to rob them of these his gifts; and he told them how to keep them safely. He told them that many would seek to make them waste what he had given to them on pleasing themselves, but that they must remember always, that what they had, belonged to him; that they would have to give him an account of their way of using all his gifts; and that he would reward with everlasting favour those who now were faithful to him. He told them also to set about trading for him as early as they could; for that all the merchants' goods were freshest in the morning; that then the precious stones were the finest and the truest; but that those who waited till the evening would find all the best goods sold; and that, perhaps, before they had anything ready, the trumpet would sound which was to call them all out of the city, and then they would have to come back to him empty-handed and disgraced.

When he had given them these charges, he sent them from his presence to begin their journey to the great city. All that day they travelled with horses and camels over plains and hills, and fruitful fields and deserts, until, just as the sun went down, they came to the walls of a great city; and they knew that it was here they were to traffic for their king upon the morrow.

Then the thoughtful servants began carefully to unpack their goods; they looked into their bales of precious stuffs to see that they had got no injury from the dust and sand of the desert; they counted over their bags of money to see that all was right; and began to lay them all in order, that they might enter the town as soon as the gates were open, and trade for their king in the morning hours, which he had told them were the best.

But some of the other servants laughed at them for taking all this care and trouble. "Surely it will be time enough," they said, "to get everything ready when the markets are open to-morrow. We have had a long, hot, weary journey, and we must rest and refresh ourselves before we think of trading." So they spread the tables, and began to feast in a riotous way, quite forgetting the King's service, and putting the morrow out of their thoughts.

Now as soon as the sun was up, in the morning, there was a great stir amongst the servants. Those who had been careful and watchful in the evening were ready with all their bales; and as soon as ever the city-gates were open, they

marched in through them with their goods. It
was a great wide city into which they entered,
and must hold, they thought, a vast multitude
of men. Houses and streets of all sizes met
their eyes here and there ; but they passed
easily along, because it was still so early in the
morning that few persons were in the streets,
and those few were all bent upon business, as
they were themselves. So they passed on to
the great market where the merchants bought
and sold, and here they set out all their goods ;
and the merchants came round them to look
over their wares, and to show them what they
had to sell in return. Now they found it true
as the king had foretold them. For they had
the first choice of all that the merchants could
offer. One of them opened his stores, and showed
them rubies, and diamonds, and pearls, such as
they had never seen before for size and beauty.
So they chose a pearl of great price, and they
bought it for their prince, and they trafficked in
their other wares, and gained for him more than
as many bags of treasure as he had given them
at first. So they traded according to their skill,
and every one had now secured something for
his lord. The pearl of great price was stored
by some ; others had rich dresses adorned with
gold and precious stones ; others had bags of

the most refined gold; others had the spices of Arabia and the frankincense of the islands of the East.

One there was amongst them who seemed to have got nothing to carry home with him; and yet he, as well as the rest, had laid out his master's gift. Then some of the other servants asked him what he had stored up for the king? and he said that he had no riches which he could show to them, but that he had an offering which he knew that the merciful heart of the King would make him love and value. Then they asked him to tell them his story; so he said that, as he was walking through the market, he had seen a poor woman weeping and wringing her hands, as if her heart would break: he stopped, and asked her the cause of her sorrow, and she told him that she was a widow, and that some merchants, to whom her husband had owed large sums of money, had come that morning to her house and taken all that she had, and seized her children too; and that they were dragging them away to the slave-market to sell them for slaves in a far land, that they might pay themselves the debt which her husband had owed them. So when he heard her sad tale, he opened his bag of treasure, and found that all the gold which he had got in it

would just pay the widow's debt and set her
children free. Then he went with her to the
merchants, and he told out to them all that sum,
and set the children of the widow free, and gave
them back to their mother; and "I am taking,"
he said, "to our merciful king the offering of the
widow's tears and gratitude; and I know that
this is an offering which will be well-pleasing in
his sight."

So it fared with these faithful servants in their
trading; and all the while they were cheerful
and light-hearted, because they remembered
constantly the love and kindness which their
king had showed to them; and they rejoiced
that they were able to serve him and to trade
for him with his gifts. They thought also of
the goodness of the king's son towards them;
they remembered how he had sought them when
they were prisoners in the dark dungeons of
their tyrant enemy; and they were full of joy
when they thought that they should be able to
offer to him the goodly pearl, or the other curious
gifts, which they had brought. They thought
of these things until they longed to hear the
trumpet sound, which was to call them out of
the town and gather them together for their
journey home. When that trumpet might sound,
they knew not; but the sun was now past its

noon, and the town, which had been so quiet when they came in the early morning along its empty streets, was now full of noise, and bustle, and confusion, as great towns are wont to be when all the multitude of sleepers awaken and pour out for pleasure, or business, or idleness, into the streets, and squares, and market-places.

Heartily glad were they now that they had been so early at their traffic. Now the merchants had shut up all their richest stores; and the markets were full of others who brought false pearls and mock diamonds, instead of the costly gems for which they had traded in the morning. There seemed to be hardly any true traders left. Idlers were there in numbers, and shows and noisy revels were passing up and down the streets; and they could see thieves and bad men lurking about at all the corners, seeking whom they could catch, and rob, and plunder.

On all these things the servants looked; sometimes they saw beautiful sights pass by them, which gladdened their eyes; and sometimes sweet music would fill their ears, as bands of merry harpers and singers walked up and down through the market; and they rejoiced in all of these, but still their hearts were full of thoughts of their kind king, and recollections of his son their prince; and they longed to be at home with them, even when the sights round them were the gayest, and the sounds in their ears were the sweetest; and they were ever watching for the voice of the trumpet, which was to call them again homeward.

But this happy case was not that of *all* the servants. When these watchful men had been entering the gates of the city in the morning, the thoughtless servants were not yet awake. They had sat up late at their feasting and rejoicings, and when the morning sun rose upon them, they were still in their first deep sleep. The stirring of their fellow-servants moved them a little, and for awhile they seemed ready to rise and join them. But their goods were not ready, so they could not go with them; and they might as well, therefore, they thought, wait a little longer and rest themselves, and then follow them to the market. They did not mean to be late, but they saw no reason why they should be so very early.

So they slept till the sun was high, and then they rose in some confusion, because it was now so late : and they had all their goods to unpack, their stuffs to smooth out, and the dust to shake off from them. Soon they began about every little thing to find fault with one another, because they were secretly angry with themselves.

THE KING AND HIS SERVANTS

Each one thought that if his neighbour had not persuaded him to stay, he should have been up, and have entered the city with the earliest; so high words arose between them; and instead of helping one another, and making the best they could of the time which remained, they only hindered one another, and made it later and later before they were ready to begin their trading.

So, after many hard words and much bad temper, one by one they got away; each as soon as he was ready, and often with his goods all in confusion; every one following his own path, and wandering by himself up the crowded streets of the full town.

Hard work they had to get at all along it when they had passed the gates. All the stream of people seemed now to be setting against them. The idlers jested upon their strange dress; and if they did but try to traffic for their lord, the rude children of the town would gather round them, and hoot, and cry; so that they could manage no trade at all.

Then, as I watched them, I saw that some who had been the loudest in talking of what they should do when they were tried, were now the first to give up altogether making any head at all against the crowd of that city. They had packed up what goods they might have, and began to think only of looking about them, and following the crowd, and pleasing themselves, like any of the men around them. Then I looked after some of these, and I saw that one of them was led on by the crowd to a place in the town where there was a great show. Outside of it were men in many-coloured dresses, who blew with trumpets, and jested, and cried aloud, and begged all to come in and see the strange sights which were stored within.

Now when the servant came to this place, he watched one and another go in, until at last he also longed to go in and see the sights which were to be gazed on within. So he went to the door, and the porter asked him for money ; but when he drew out his purse, and the porter saw that his money belonged to some strange place, and was quite unlike the coin used in that town, he only laughed at it, and said it was good for nothing there, and bid him "stand back." So as he turned away, the porter saw the rich bundle on his back, and then he spoke to him in another tone, and he said, "I will let you in, if you like to give me that bundle of goods." Then for a moment the servant was checked. He thought of his lord, and of the reckoning, and he remembered the words, "As good stewards of the

manifold grace of God"; and he had almost
determined to turn back, and to fight his way
to the market-place, and to trade for his lord,
let it cost him what it might. But just at the
moment there was a great burst of the showman's
trumpets; and he heard the people shouting for
joy within; and so he forgot all but his great
desire, and slipping off the bundle from his
shoulders, he put it into the hands of the porter,
and passed in, and I saw him no more.

Then I saw another, who was standing at the
corner of a street gazing at some strange antics
which were being played by a company of the
townsmen. And as he gazed upon them, he
forgot all about his trading for his master, and
thought only of seeing more of this strange sight.
Then I saw that whilst he was thinking only of
these follies, some evil-minded men gathered
round him, and before he was aware of it, they
secretly stole from him all the gold which his
lord had given him to lay out for him. The
servant did not even know when it was gone,
so much was he thinking of staring at the sight
before him. But it made me very sad to think
that when he went to buy for his master, he
would find out, too late, his loss; and that when
the trumpet sounded, he would have nothing to
carry back with him on the day of reckoning.

THE KING AND HIS SERVANTS

Some of these loiterers, too, were treated even worse than this. One of them I saw whom the shows and lights of that town led on from street to street, until he came quite to its farther end; and then he thought that he saw before him, beyond some lonely palings, still finer sights than any he had left; and so he set out to cross over those fields, and see those sights. And when he was half over, some wicked robbers, who laid wait in those desolate places, rushed out upon him from their lurking-place, and ill-used him sorely, and robbed him of all his goods and money, and left him upon the ground, hardly able to get back to the town which he had left.

Then I saw one of these loiterers who, as he was looking idly at the sights round him, grew very grave, and began to tremble from head to foot. One of his fellows, who stood by and saw him, quickly asked him what made him tremble. At first he could not answer; but after a while he said, that the sound of the trumpet which they had just heard had made him think of the great trumpet-sound of their master, which was to call them all back to his presence, and that he trembled because the evening was coming on, and he had not yet traded for his lord. And "How," he said in great fear, "how shall we ever stand that reckoning with our hands empty?"

Then some of his companions in idleness laughed and jeered greatly at him, and mocked the poor trembler. But his fears were wiser than their mockings; and so, it seemed, he knew, for he cared nothing for them; but only said to them, very sadly and gravely, "You are in the same danger, how then can you jeer at me?" And with that he pointed their eyes up to the sky, and showed them how low the sun had got already, and that it wanted but an hour at the most to his setting, and then that the trumpet might sound at any moment, and they have nothing to bear home to their lord.

Now, as he spoke, one listened eagerly to him; and whilst the others jeered, he said very gravely, "What can we do? Is it quite too late?" "It is never too late," said the other, "till the trumpet sounds; and though we have lost so much of the day, perchance we can yet do something; come with me to the market-place, and we will try." So the other joined him, and off they set, passing through their companions, who shouted after them all the way they went, until the townsmen who stood round began to jeer and shout after them also; so that all the town was moved. A hard time those two had now, and much they wished that they had gone to the market-place in the early morning, when

the streets were empty, and the busy servants
had passed so easily along. Many were the
rough words they had now to bear; many the
angry or ill-natured crowd through which they
had to push; and if anywhere they met one of
their late and idle companions, he was sure to
stir up all the street against them, when he saw
them pushing on to the market-place.

"Do you think that we shall ever get there?"
said he who had been moved by the other's words
to him who led the way and buffeted with the
crowd, like a man swimming through many rough
waves in the strong stream of some swift river.
"Do you think that we shall ever get there?"
"Yes, yes," said the other; "we shall get there
still, if we do but persevere." "But it is so hard
to make any way, and the streets seem to grow
fuller and fuller; I am afraid that I shall never
get through."

Just as he spoke, a great band of the towns-
people, with music, and trumpets, and dancing,
met them like a mighty wave of the sea, and
seemed sure to drive them back ; one of their old
companions was dancing amongst the rest; and
as I looked hard at him, I saw that it was the
same who had given away his precious burden in
order to go into the show. Now, as soon as he
saw these his former fellows, he called to them

by their names, and bade them join him and the townsmen round him. But he that was leading the way shook his head, and said boldly, "No; we will not join with you; we are going to the market-place to traffic for our lord." "It is too late for that," said he; "you lost the morning, and now you cannot trade." Then I saw that he who before had trembled exceedingly, grew very pale; but still he held on his way; and he said, "Yes, we have lost the morning, and a sore thing it is for us; but our good lord will help us even yet; and we WILL serve him, redeeming the time, because the days are evil." Then he turned to the other and said to him, "And will not you stop either? Do not be fooled by this madman; what use is it to go to buy when the shops are all shut, and the market empty?" Then he hung down his head, and looked as though he would have turned back, and fallen into the throng; but his fellow seized him by the hand, and bid him take courage, and think upon his kind master, and upon the king's son, whose very blood had been shed for them; and with that he seemed to gather a little confidence, and held on for a while in his way with the other.

Then their old companion turned all his seeming love into hatred, and he called upon the crowd round him to lay hands on them and stop them; and so it would fain have done, but that, as it seemed to me, a power greater than their own was with those servants, and strengthened them; until they pushed the rude people aside on the right and on the left, and passed safely through them into another street.

Here there were fewer persons, and they had a breathing-time for a while; and as they heard the sound of music and of the crowd passing by at some little distance from them, they began to gather heart, and to talk to one another. "I never thought," said the one, "that I could have held on through that crowd; and I never could, if you had not stretched out your hand to help me." "Say, rather, if our master's strength had not been with us," said the other. "But do you think," said the other, "that he will accept anything we can bring him now, when the best part of the day is over?" "Yes, I do," he replied. "I have a good hope that he will; for I remember how he said, 'Return, ye backsliding children, return ye even unto me.'" "But how can one who is so trembling and fearful as I am ever traffic for him?" "You can, if you will but hold on; for he has once spoken of his servants as 'faint yet pursuing.'" "Well," said the other, "I wish that I had your courage; but I do believe that I should not dare to meet such another crowd as that we have just passed through; I really thought that they would tear us in pieces." "Our king will never let that be," said the other, "if only we trust in him." "But are you sure," replied he, "that our king does see us in this town?"

Now, before his companion had time to answer him again, they heard a louder noise than ever, of men dancing and singing, and crowding, and music playing, and horns blowing, as if all the mad sports of the city were coming upon them in one burst. At the front of all they could see their old companion; for the band had turned round by a different street, and now were just beginning to come down that one up which they were passing. Then he who had been affrighted before, turned white as snow; and he looked this way and that, to see what he could do.

Now it so happened, that just by where they stood was a great shop, and in its windows there seemed to shine precious stones and jewels, and fine crystals, and gold and ivory. So, as he looked, his eyes fell full upon the shop, and he said to his fellow, "Look here; surely here is what we want; let us turn in here and traffic for our master, and then we shall escape all this rout which is coming upon us." "No, no!" said the other; "we must push on to the market; that is our appointed place; there our lord bids us trade;

we must not turn aside from the trouble which
our lateness has brought upon us—we must not
offer to our master that which costs us nothing.
Play the man, and we shall soon be in the market."
"But we shall be torn in pieces," said the other.
"Look at the great crowd; and even now it seems
that our old companion sees me, and is beginning
to lead the rabble upon us." "Never fear," said
he who led the way; "our king will help us.
'I will not be afraid for ten thousands of the
people who have set themselves against us round
about.'"

Then I saw that he to whom he spoke did not
seem to hear these last words, for the master of
the shop had noticed how he cast his eyes upon
the goods that were in the window; and so he
came to the door, and begged him to come in.
"Come in, come in," he said, "before the crowd
sweep you away; come in and buy my pearls, and
my diamonds, and my precious stones; come in,
come in." Now, while he halted for a moment
to parley with the man, the crowd came upon
them, and he was parted from his friend, who had
held up his fainting steps; and so he sprung
trembling into the shop, scarcely thinking himself
safe even there.

Now the man into whose house he had turned,
though he was a fair-spoken man, and one who

knew well how to seem honest and true, was altogether a deceiver. All his seeming jewels, and diamonds, and pearls, were but shining and painted glass, which was worth nothing at all to him who was so foolish as to buy it; but this the servant knew not. If it had been in the bright clear light of the morning, he would easily have seen that the diamonds and the pearls were only sparkling and painted glass, and the gold nothing but tinsel; but the bright light of the morning had passed away, and in the red slanting light of the evening sun he could not see clearly; and so the false man persuaded him, and he parted with all the rich treasures which his king had given him, and got nothing for them in exchange which was worth the having, for he filled his bag with bits of painted glass, which his lord would never accept.

However, he knew not how he had been cheated; or if, perhaps, a thought crossed his mind that all was not right, it was followed by another, which said that it was now too late to alter, and that if he had chosen wrongly, still he must abide by it: and so he waited for the trumpet. But he was not altogether happy; and often and often he wished that he had faced the strife of the multitude, and pressed on with his trusting companion to the market.

A hard struggle had been his before he had

reached it. It seemed indeed at times as if the words of his fearful companion were coming true, and he would be torn altogether to pieces, so fiercely did the crowd press upon him and throng him. But as I watched him in the thickest part of it, I saw that always, just at his last need, something seemed to favour him, and the crowd broke off and left room for him to struggle by. I could hear him chanting, as it were, to himself, when the crowd looked upon him the most fiercely, "I will not be afraid for ten thousands of the people that have set themselves against me round about." And even as he chanted the words, the crowd divided itself in two parts, like a rushing stream sliding by some black rock; and on he passed, as though they saw him not.

So it continued, even till he reached the market-place. Right glad was he to find himself there; but even now all his trials were not over. Many of the stalls were empty, and from many more the fair and true traders were gone away; and instead of them were come false and deceitful men, who tried to put off any who dealt with them with pretended jewels and bad goods.

Then did he look anxiously round and round the market, fearing every moment lest the trumpet should sound before he had purchased anything for his lord. Never, perhaps, all along the way, did he so bitterly regret his early sloth as now, for he wrung his hands together, and said in great bitterness, "What shall I do?" and "How shall I, a loiterer, traffic for my lord?"

Then his eyes fell upon a shop where were no jewels, nor gold, nor costly silks, nor pearls of great price; but all that was in it was coarse sackcloth, and rough and hairy garments, and heaps of ashes, and here and there a loaf of bitter bread, and bitter herbs, and bottles wherein tears were stored. As he gazed on this shop, something seemed to whisper to his heart, "Go and buy." So he went with his sorrowful heart, as one not worthy to traffic for his master, and he bought the coarsest sackcloth, and the ashes of affliction, and many bitter tears; and so he waited for the sounding of the trumpet.

Then suddenly, as some loud noise breaks upon the slumbers of men who sleep, that great trumpet sounded. All through the air came its voice, still waxing louder and louder; and even as it pealed across the sky, all that great city, and its multitudes, and its lofty palaces, and its show, and its noise, and its revels, all melted away, and were not. And in a moment all the servants were gathered together, and their lord and king stood amongst them. All else was gone, and they and their works were alone with him.

Then was there a fearful trial of every man's work. Then were they crowned with light and gladness who had risen early and traded diligently, and who now brought before their master the fruit of that toil, and labour, and pain. Each one had his own reward; and amongst the richest and the best—as though he brought what the king greatly loved—was his reward who brought unto his master the offerings of gratitude from the broken-hearted widow.

Then drew near the servant who had wasted the morning, but had repented of his sloth, and had fought his way through the crowds, and had at last bought the sackcloth. So he drew near with it; and it looked poor, and mean, and coarse, as he bore it amongst the heaps of gold, and jewels, and silks, which lay piled up all around; yet did he draw near unto the king; and as he came, he spoke and said, "A broken and a contrite heart wilt thou not despise." And as he spake, the king looked graciously upon him; a mild and an approving smile sat upon his countenance, and he spoke to him also the blessed words, "Well done, thou good and faithful servant." Then did the coarse sackcloth shine as the most rich cloth of gold; then did the ashes of the furnace sparkle as a monarch's jewels; whilst every bitter tear which was stored in the bottle changed into pearls and rubies which were above all price.

Then the king turned to the careless servants, and his voice was terrible to hear, and from his face they fled away. I dared not to look upon them ; but I heard their just and most terrible sentence, and I knew that they were driven away for ever from the presence of the king, in which is life and peace ; and that they were bound under chains and darkness, deeper and more dreadful than those from which the king's son had graciously delivered them.

THE PROPHET'S GUARD

[2 Kings vi 8—17]

IT was the very earliest morning. The day was not breaking, as it does in this land of England, with a dewy twilight and a gradual dawning—first a dull glow all over the east, then blood-red rays, catching any fleecy cloud which is stealing over the sky, and turning all its misty whiteness into gold and fire;—but day was breaking as it does in those eastern countries—sudden, and bright, and hot. Darkness flew away as at a word; the thick shadows were all at once gone, and the broad glaring sun rose proudly in the sky, rejoicing in his strength. The people of the town woke up again to life and business. Doors were flung wide open, and some were passing through them; the flat roofs of the houses began to be peopled—on one was a man praying, on others two or three standing together; but most of them were hastening here and there to get through their necessary work before the full heat of the day came on; numbers were passing and repassing to the clear dancing fountain, whose cool waters bubbled up in the midst of a broad square within that city.

And now, what is it which one suddenly sees, and, after gazing at it for awhile, points out to another, and he to a third? As each hears, they look eagerly up to the hill, which rises high above their town, until they gather into a knot; and then, as one and another are added to their company, grow into almost a crowd. Still it is in the same quarter that all eyes are fixed; their water-vessels are set idly down, as if they could not think of them. Those which were set under the fountain have been quite full this long time, but no one stooped to remove them; and the water has been running over their brimming sides, while its liquid silver flew all round in a shower of sparkling drops. But no one thinks of them. What is it which so chains all eyes and fixes the attention of all?

The hill is quite full of armed men. There were none there overnight; they have come up from the vale silently and stealthily during the darkness, while men slept; and like some great mist rising from the waters, they seem to be hemming in the town on every side. Look which way you will, the sun lights upon the burnished and brilliant points of spears, or falls on strong shields, or flashes like lightning from polished and cutting swords, or is thrown a thousand ways by the rolling wheels of those war-chariots. "Who are they?" is the question of all; and no one likes to say what all have felt for a long time—"They are our enemies, and we are their prey."

But there is no use shutting the eyes any longer to the truth. The morning breeze has just floated off in its waves that flag which before hung down lifelessly by the side of its staff. It has shewn all. They are enemies; they are fierce and bitter enemies; they are the Syrians, and they are at war with Israel.

But why are they come against this little town? When they have licked up it and its people like the dust from the face of the earth, they will be scarcely further on in their war against Israel. Why did not they begin with some of the great and royal cities? Why was it not against Jerusalem, or Jezreel, or even against the newly-rebuilt Jericho? Why should they come against this little town?

Then one, an evil-looking man of a dark countenance, one who feared not God and loved not his servants, whispered to those around him, and said, "Have you not heard how Elisha the prophet, who dwells amongst us, has discovered to the king of Israel the secrets of the army of the king of

Syria? No doubt it is because Elisha is dwelling
here that the king of Syria has come upon us.
And now shall we, and our wives, and our sweet
babes, and our houses, and our treasures, become
the prey of the king of Syria, for the sake of this
Elisha. I always thought that no good would
come from his dwelling here."

Now, fear makes men cruel and suspicious,
and fills their minds with hard thoughts; and
many of these men were full of fear; and so,
when they heard these words, they began to have
hard bad thoughts of God's prophet, and to hate
him as the cause of all the evils which they were
afraid would very soon come upon them.

Just then the door of another house opened:
it was the prophet's house, and his servant came
forth with the water-vessels to fill them at the
fountain. He wondered to see the crowd of men
gathered together, and he drew near to ask them
what was stirring. He could read upon their
dark scowling faces that something moved them
exceedingly; but what it was he could not gather.
He could not tell why they would scarcely speak
to him, but looked on him with angry faces, and
spoke under their breath, and said, "This is one
of them." "'Twere best to give them up." "They
will destroy us all." Then the man was altogether
astonished ; for his master had been ever humble

and kind and gentle; no poor man had ever turned away without help when he had come in his sorrows to the prophet of the Lord. And yet, why were they thus angry with him, if it were not for his master's sake?

Broken sentences were all that he could gather; but, by little and little, he learned what they feared and what they threatened; he saw, also, the hosts of armed men gathered all around the city; and his heart, also, was filled with fear. He believed that it was for his master's sake that they were there; he saw that all around him were turned against his master, and he trembled exceedingly. For some time he stood amongst the rest, scarce knowing what to do, neither liking to remain nor daring to go; until at last, as some more stragglers joined themselves to the company, he slunk away like one ashamed, without stopping even to fill the water-vessels he had brought.

And so he entered his own door, heavy-hearted and trembling; and he went to the prophet's chamber, for he deemed that he still slept. But the man of God was risen; and he knew, therefore, where he should find him—that he would be upon the flat roof of his house, calling upon the name of the Lord his God, who had made another morning's sun to rise in its glory.

So he followed his master to the house-top;

and there, even as he had supposed, he found the holy man. It was a striking sight, could any one have seen the difference between these two men— the one pale and trembling and affrighted, like a man out of himself, and with no stay on which to rest his mind; the other calm and earnest, as, in deep and solemn prayer, with his head bowed and his hands clasped together, his low voice poured forth his thanksgiving, or spake of his needs; he also, as it seemed, was out of himself, but going out of himself that he might rest upon One who was near to him though his eye saw Him not, and who spake to him though his outward ear heard no voice of words.

Thus he continued for a season, as if he knew not that any man was nigh unto him; as if he knew not that there were, in the great world around him, any one besides his God with whom he communed, and his own soul which spake unto his God. All this time his servant stood by him, pale and trembling, but not daring to break in upon that hour of prayer: until at length the prophet paused, and his eye fell upon the trembler; and he turned towards him, and said kindly, "What ails thee, my son?" Then the servant answered, "Oh, my father, look unto the hill." And he stood gazing in the prophet's face, as though he expected to see paleness and terror overspread it when his eyes gathered in the sight of those angry hosts. But it was not so. No change passed over his countenance; his brow was open as it was before; the colour never left his cheeks; and, with almost a smile, he turned unto the servant, and said, "And why does this affright thee?" "It is for thee they seek, my father—it is for thee they seek; and the wicked men of the town are ready to fall upon thee and deliver thee into their hands. Even now, as I walked along the street, they looked on me with fierce and cruel eyes; and they breathed threats which these lips may not utter, and said, that thou hadst brought this trouble upon them and their wives and their little ones; and I feared that they would curse thee and thy God." But the prophet was not moved by his words, for he only answered, "Fear them not; they that are with us are more than they that are against us." Then did the servant cast his eyes to the ground, and he spake not, yet his lips moved; and if any one had heard the words which he whispered, they might perhaps have heard him ask how this could be, when they were but two, and their enemies were so many and so mighty.

Now the prophet's eye rested upon him, and he read all his secret thoughts; and he pitied his weakness, for that holy man was full of pity for

the weak; so he chid him not; but, bowing his
knees again on that flat roof, he prayed unto his
God to open those eyes which earthly fear had
darkened. His prayer was heard. For there
fell from them as it were films; and now, when
he looked out, he saw a glorious sight. All the
mountain was full; and they were a wonderful
company which filled it. The dark hosts of the
Syrians, and their glancing swords and clashing
chariots, now looked but as a mere handful; for
the whole mountain round them was full of that
terrible army. Chariots of fire and horsemen of
fire thronged it in every part. High up into the
viewless air mounted their wheeling bands; rank
beyond rank, and army beyond army, they seemed
to stretch on into the vastness of space, until his
wearied eye was unable to gaze on them. And
all of these were gathered round his master.
They were God's host, keeping guard over God's
servant. And they who would injure him must
first turn aside those flashing swords, must break
up that strong and serried array, and be able
to do battle with God's mighty angels.

Then was the weak heart strong. Then did
the poor trembler see that he was safe; and
know that he who is on God's side can never
want companions and defenders.

THE BROTHERS' MEETING;

OR, THE SINS OF YOUTH

[Genesis xxxii 3—21, xxxiii 1—16]

A LARGE company was winding its way slowly out of the vale in which the river Jordan runs. The sun was just beginning to strike hotly upon them, and make them long for rest and shelter, as they toiled up the open sandy hills and amongst the great masses of rock with which that country was strewn.

It was a striking sight to see those travellers. First went three troops of kine, lowing as they went ; camels with their arched necks, stooping shoulders, and forward ears ; asses with their foals; ewes and lambs ; and goats with their kids, which mounted idly upon every rock that lay by their road-side, and then jumped as idly down again ; and before and after these, drivers in stately turbans and long-flowing robes, keeping the flocks and herds to their appointed way. Then came large droves of cattle, and sheep, and goats, and asses, stirring up with their many feet the dust of the sandy plain till it fell like a gentle shower, powdering with its small grains all the rough and prickly plants which grew in tufts over the waste. Then there was a space, and after that were seen two bands of camels— the best they seemed to be of all the flock, those which came last especially—and on them were children and women riding, over whom hung long veils to shelter their faces from the hot breath of the sandy desert through which they had travelled. And after all these came one man, with a staff in his hand and a turban on his head, walking slowly, as one who walked in pain and yet walked on, following those who went before.

If you had stood near to that man, you might, perhaps, have heard him speaking to God in prayer and thanksgiving; you might have heard him saying to himself, "with my staff passed I over this Jordan, and now I am become two bands"; or you might have heard him earnestly calling upon the God of Abraham, and the God of Isaac, his father, to keep him safe in the great danger which now lay close before him. His mind was certainly very full of that danger, for he kept looking up from the sand on which his eyes were often fixed, and gazing as far as he

could see over the hills before him, as if he
expected to see some great danger suddenly meet
him on his way, and as if, therefore, he wished to
be quite ready for it.

If you looked into his face, you could see at
once that he was not a common man. He was
not a very old man; his hair was not yet grey
upon his head; and yet it seemed, when you
looked first at him, as if he was very old. But
as you looked closer, you saw that it was not so;
but that his face seemed to speak of many, many
thoughts which had passed through his mind,
and left those deep marks stamped even on his
face. It was not only sorrow, though there was
much of that; or care, though he was now full
of care; but besides these, it seemed as if he had
seen, and done, and felt great things—things in
which all a man's soul is called up, and so, even
when they have passed away again, leave some
of their impressions stamped upon the face.

He HAD seen great things, and felt great
things. He had seen God's most holy angels
going up to heaven, and coming down to earth
upon their messages of mercy. He had heard
the voice of the Lord of all, promising to be his
Father and his Friend. And only the night
before, the Angel of the Covenant had made
himself known to him in the stillness of his lonely

tent, and made him strong to wrestle with him for a blessing, until the breaking of the day. So that it was no wonder, that when you looked into his face, it was not like the face of a common man, but one which was full of thought, which bore almost outwardly the stamp of great mysteries.

But what was it which now filled this man with care? He was returning home from a far land where he had been staying twenty years, to the land where his father dwelt. He had gone out a poor man; he was coming home a rich man. He was bringing back with him his wives, and his children, and his servants, and his flocks, and his herds; and of what was he afraid? Surely he could trust the God who had kept him and blessed him all these twenty years, and who had led him now so far on his journey?

Why should he fear now, when he was almost at his father's tent?

It was because he heard that HIS BROTHER was coming to meet him. But why should this fill him with such fear? Surely it would be a happy meeting; brothers born of the same father and of the same mother, who had dwelt together in one tent, kneeled before one father's knees in prayer, and joined together in the common plays of childhood—surely their meeting must be happy, now that they have been twenty years asunder, and God had blessed them both, and they were about to see each other again in peace and safety, and to shew each other the children whom God had given them, and who must remind them of their days of common childhood. And why then is the man afraid? Because when he left his father's house this brother was very angry with him, and he fears that he may have remembered his anger all these twenty years, and be ready now to revenge himself for that old quarrel.

And yet, why should this make such an one to fear? Even if his brother be still angry with him, and have cruel and evil thoughts against him, cannot God deliver him?—cannot the same God who has kept him safely all these twenty years of toil and labour, help and save him now? Why, then, does he fear so greatly? He has not forgotten that this God can save him—he has not for a moment forgotten it; for see how earnestly he makes his prayers unto Him; hear his vows that if God will again deliver him, he and all of his shall ever praise and serve Him for this mercy. Yet still he is in fear; and he seems like a man who thought that there was some reason why the God who had heard him in other cases should not hear him in this.

What was it, then, which pressed so heavily

upon this man's mind? It was the remembrance
of an old sin. He feared that God would leave
him now to Esau's wrath, because he knew that
Esau's wrath was God's punishment of his sin.
He feared that Esau's hand would slay his
children, as God's chastisement for the sins of
his childhood. He remembered that he had lied
to Isaac his father, and mocked the dimness of
his aged eyes by a false appearance; now he
trembled lest his father's God should leave the
deceiver and the mocker to eat the bitter fruit
of his old sin. It was not so much Esau's wrath,
and Esau's company, and Esau's arms which he
feared—though all these were very terrible to this
peaceful man—as it was his own sin in days long
past, which now met him again, and seemed to
frown upon him from the darkness before him.
In vain did he strive to look on and see whether
God would guide him there, for his sin clouded
over the light of God's countenance. It was as
when he strained his eyes into the great sand-
drifts of the desert through which he had passed;
they danced and whirled fearfully before him,
and baffled all the strivings of his eager eyes.

But the time of trial was drawing very near.
And how did it end? Instead of falling upon him
and slaying him and his; instead of making a
spoil of the oxen, and the asses, and the camels,

and giving the young children to the sword, Esau's heart melted as soon as they met; he fell upon his brother's neck and kissed him; he looked lovingly upon the children who had been born to him in the far land; he spake kindly of the old days of their remembered childhood, of the grey-haired man at home; and he would not take even the present which his brother had set apart for him.

Jacob knew who it was that had turned his brother's heart, and he felt more than ever what a strong and blessed thing prayer and supplication was. Nor did he forget his childhood's sin against his God. It had looked out again upon him in manhood, and reminded him of God's holiness, of his many past misdeeds, and made him pray more earnestly not to be made to "possess the iniquities of his youth."

For EU product safety concerns, contact us at Calle de José Abascal, 56–1°,
28003 Madrid, Spain or eugpsr@cambridge.org.

www.ingramcontent.com/pod-product-compliance
Ingram Content Group UK Ltd.
Pitfield, Milton Keynes, MK11 3LW, UK
UKHW012331130625
459647UK00009B/205